But Who Am I, And Who Are My People?

A Rabbi's Reflections on the Rabbinate and the Jewish Community

But Who Am I, And Who Are My People?

A Rabbi's Reflections on the Rabbinate and the Jewish Community

by

Rabbi Marc D. Angel

Ktav Publishing House, Inc.

Copyright© 2001
Marc D. Angel

Library of Congress Cataloging-in-Publication Data

Angel, Marc.
  But who am I, and who are my people? : a rabbi's reflections on the rabbinate and the Jewish community / by Marc D. Angel.
  p. cm.
ISBN 0-88125694-3
  1. Rabbis--United States--Office. 2. Jewish way of life. 3. Judaism--United States. 4. Angel, Marc. I. Title.

BM652 .A54 2001
296.6'1--dc21

00-046963

Distributed by
Ktav Publishing House, Inc.
900 Jefferson Street
Hoboken, NJ 07030
201-963-9524 FAX 201-963-0102
Email ktav@compuserve.com

Contents

Acknowledgments ix

Introduction xv

1. Malkhut—Kingdom 1

2. Netsah—Endurance 15

3. Hod—Splendor, Majesty 37

4. Yesod—Foundation 55

5. Ḥesed—Compassion 71

6. Gevurah—Strength, Heroism 89

7. Tiferet—Splendor, Glory 105

8. Binah—Discernment 125

9. Ḥokhmah—Wisdom 145

10. Keter—Crown 165

Epilogue 177

Bibliography 179

In honor and in appreciation of my parents-in-law,
Rabbi Paul and Dorothy Schuchalter,
Bearers of a many-generational rabbinic tradition

Acknowledgments

This book is the result of over thirty years of experience as a rabbi. It owes its existence to a wide array of people—family, teachers, congregants, colleagues, students, friends and acquaintances.

I thank the leadership and members of Congregation Shearith Israel, with which I have been associated since 1969. I express a special word of gratitude to the current officers of the Congregation: Mr. Alvin Deutsch, Parnas-President; Mr. Peter Neustadter and Mr. David J. Nathan, Seganim-Vice Presidents.

It is my pleasure to thank Mr. Bernard Scharfstein and his staff at Ktav Publishing House for their commitment to this project. Indeed, the idea for writing this book came from Bernard. I thank Mrs. Jean Naggar for her efforts on behalf of this book.

To my wife, Gilda, and to our children and grandchildren—words are not adequate to express my love, respect and appreciation.

I thank the Almighty for having brought us to this special moment.

Rabbi Marc D. Angel
Menahem Ab 15, 5760

First Chronicles 29:9–15

Then the people rejoiced, for that they offered willingly, because with a whole heart they offered willingly to the Lord; and David the king also rejoiced with great joy.

Wherefore David blessed the Lord before all the congregation; and David said: Blessed be Thou, O Lord, the God of Israel our father, for ever and ever. Thine, O Lord, is the greatness and the power and the glory and the victory and the majesty; for all that is in the heaven and in the earth is Thine; Thine is the kingdom, O Lord, and Thou art exalted as head above all. Both riches and honor come of Thee, and Thou rulest over all; and in Thy hand is power and might; and in Thy hand it is to make great, and to give strength unto all. Now, therefore, our God, we thank Thee and praise Thy glorious name.

But who am I, and who are my people, that we should be able to offer so willingly as this? For all things come of Thee, and of Thine own have we given Thee. For we are strangers before Thee, and sojourners, as all our ancestors were: our days on the earth are as a shadow, and there is no abiding.

The Sefirot (Divine Emanations)

Keter—Crown

Binah—Discernment   Ḥokhmah—Wisdom

Tiferet—Splendor, Glory

Gevurah—Strength, Heroism   Ḥesed—Compassion

Yesod—Foundation

Hod—Splendor, Majesty   Netsaḥ—Endurance

Malkhut—Kingdom

Introduction

In the winter of 1999, Bernard Scharfstein of Ktav Publishing House asked me to write a book on the nature of the rabbinic life. Perhaps a diary. Perhaps a memoir. Whatever I thought would help people to better understand the world of rabbis.

I pondered the idea for several months. A diary? A memoir? These seemed too self-serving and even egotistical. And although I have been serving as a rabbi for thirty years, I still feel that I am too young to write a book of memoirs. There are miles to go before I rest, miles to go. I am not ready to stand atop the mountain of time and look back, nostalgically, at the span of my career. I am still in the midst of this career, moving along at full pace.

But Bernard's suggestion kept tempting me. I went through my files, going back to the beginning of my service as rabbi in 1969. I looked through sermons, essays, and books I have written over the years. I combed through decades of correspondence, newspaper clippings, programs. I even began to organize the material into broad categories that might ultimately become chapters of a book on my life as a rabbi.

But I finally decided that I was not ready or able to write such a book. Instead, the idea came to me to write a book on Jewish thought and contemporary life, based on what I have learned and experienced during my thirty years as a rabbi. This would not be an autobiography, but would be based in large measure on what I have thought and done during my years as a rabbi. So it might serve to help the general public gain a better insight into the rabbinical life; and, at the same time, be a way of sharing what I have learned with others about the contemporary American Jewish experience.

I did not always think that I would become a rabbi. I was born and raised in Seattle, as were my parents. My maternal grandparents had come as teenagers to Seattle from Turkey during the first decade of the twentieth century. They met and were married in Seattle. My paternal grandparents came to Seattle about the same time from the Island of Rhodes. All four of my grandparents were Sephardic Jews, and Judeo-Spanish was their mother tongue. They were good, hard-working people, for whom religious tradition was important. Both of my grandfathers were active in their synagogues; Bohor Yehuda Angel served some years as sexton and Hebrew teacher of Congregation Ezra Bessaroth, and Marco Romey was active in (and at one time president of) the Sephardic Bikur Holim congregation. My paternal grandmother, Bulissa Esther Angel, gave birth to and raised eight children; my maternal grandmother, Sultana Romey, gave birth to and raised seven children. While the actual levels of religious knowledge and observance varied among family members, all took their Jewishness as a basic component of their lives.

My mother's family was far more traditionally religious than my father's family. One of my mother's sisters, Sarah, had married Rabbi Solomon Maimon, who was rabbi of the Sephardic Bikur Holim for many years. Rabbi Maimon was one of the founders of the Seattle Hebrew Day School, which I attended through eighth grade. In reflecting back on our extended family, I think that the positive religious influences of grandparents, parents, and uncles and aunts must have been pervasive. Among the twelve male cousins on my maternal side, six earned rabbinical degrees. One female cousin married a rabbi. So seven of my twenty cousins were involved in the rabbinical world, most of them primarily in Jewish education.

Upon my completion of eighth grade at the Seattle Hebrew Day School (the school did not have higher grades in those days), I attended Sharples Junior High School for ninth grade and Franklin High School for tenth through twelfth grades. The public school experience was very valuable for my intellectual and social growth, and I remain thoroughly grateful to my parents for not having sent me to a yeshiva back east for my high school years. The rabbis of the community did their best to convince parents to send their sons to yeshivot in Cleveland, Chicago, Baltimore, or New York; and a number of fellow Seattleites did pursue their high school studies at out-of-town schools. But my parents (and I) resisted the pressure, and I had the opportunity to be part of the American mainstream during my high school years.

Upon graduation from Franklin High School, I enrolled in Yeshiva College in New York. I well remember the day in early September 1963 when my parents brought me to the airport in Seattle to see me off to New York. I had never been on an airplane before. I had never been away from home for more than several weeks. And now a new life was opening up for me. I was ready and eager for the challenge, but never stopped longing for home. It was such a wonderful home, the source of so many lasting memories.

I majored in English literature and hoped I would go on to graduate school for a doctorate. My goal was to become an English professor on the college level, and devote myself to teaching and writing. In my senior year of college, I became engaged to Gilda Schuchalter, whom I had first met when we were freshmen in college. She was the president of the debating society of Stern College, and I was president of the Yeshiva College debating society. Gilda, who was the daughter of a rabbi and whose ancestors had been rabbis for generations, going back to the famous Rabbi Levi Yitzhak of Berdichev, was quite content that I wished to pursue studies in English literature. Neither of us had planned a life in the rabbinate.

During my senior year at Yeshiva College, Haham Dr. Solomon Gaon, the chief Sephardic rabbi of the Spanish and Portuguese congregations of Great Britain, was teaching there, and I was one of his students. He took me aside one day and began trying to persuade me to study for the rabbinate. There was a great need, he said, for rabbis in America, especially Sephardic rabbis. Few Sephardic students were entering the rabbinic field; who then would lead the Sephardic congregations? Who would tend to Sephardic spiritual interests? I told him that I was planning to go to graduate school in English literature. He said that was fine: and that the program of rabbinical studies at Yeshiva would allow me the opportunity to attend graduate school in English as well. I could drink from both wells of wisdom.

After discussing the question often and at length, Gilda and I decided we would follow Haham Gaon's suggestion. I enrolled in the rabbinical program of Yeshiva and the graduate school of English literature at City College.

During the spring term of my second year of rabbinical school, Haham Gaon informed me that Congregation Shearith Israel, the historic Spanish and Portuguese Synagogue of New York City, founded in 1654, was seeking a student rabbi to begin the coming autumn. I had taught in Shearith Israel's Sunday school during my senior year of college, and Gilda and I had also attended services there from time to time. Haham Gaon asked: "Would you be interested in interviewing for this position?" Yes, of course! This was an opportunity that could not be passed up. Gilda and I were filled with eager anticipation. When the position was offered to us, we could not have been happier. At that time, we were expecting our first child; the new position could not have been offered at a better time.

In September 1969 I began serving Shearith Israel. I sat on the tebah (reader's desk) next to the rabbi emeritus, Dr. David de Sola Pool; and across from Dr. Louis C. Gerstein, rabbi, and Rev. A. Lopes Cardozo, hazzan. I have been sitting in that same seat now for thirty years. I have watched our own family grow. Our son Hayyim, who was born the month after I began service at Shearith Israel, now sits next to me on the tebah as assistant rabbi of Shearith Israel. I have participated in the life of the congregation on a daily basis for all these years. I have known three, four, and in some cases five generations of families associated with Shearith Israel. The congregation has been our extended family.

When Gilda and I began our life at Shearith Israel in 1969, we still had in mind the possibility that I would eventually go on to a career in English literature. Indeed, I did earn a master's degree in English from City College.

And yet, when it came time to decide between a life in the rabbinate and a life in academia, we came down on the side of the rabbinate. Two roads diverged in the woods, and we chose the one less traveled; and that has made all the difference.

* * *

When Rabbi Joseph B. Soloveitchik eulogized Dr. Samuel Belkin, who served as president of Yeshiva University until his death in 1976, he stated that a person's life could be described as a response to two different questions: what and why? What was a person? He accomplished such-and-such; he accumulated x amount of property, published y amount of books and articles. He served in z position for *abc* years and earned *def* awards. What a person was can be culled from a resume of his achievements.

Who was a person? This is a different sort of question. The data on a resume reveal what a person was, but not *who* he was. They do not reveal the innermost aspects of the person: what did he think, feel, fear, love? Who was this person in his own eyes, in the eyes of God? While it may be interesting to know what a person was (or is), it is far more significant to know who he was (or is).

This book reveals partial answers to both what and who the author is. It is not a record of accomplishments and failures, nor is it a heart-wrenching confession or an *apologia pro vita sua*. It is an attempt to present insights into Jewish life from the vantage point of an active, long-serving Orthodox rabbi. It focuses on ideas and public experiences; it tries to maintain the personal privacy that everyone, even a rabbi, needs and deserves.

As a framework for this book, I have drawn on Kabbalistic symbolism—the ten sefirot (divine emanations) through which the Almighty created and sustains the world. Each of the sefirot has its own unique nature; together, they are the symbolic ladder linking God with His creations. Some kabbalists have arranged the sefirot in such a way as to form a picture of Adam Kadmon, primordial man. This schema relates to the "personality" of the Eternal. But in some sense, it also relates to the personality of human beings: it speaks to the issue of who we are at essence and in the ideal. In describing God's "qualities", the sefirot also serve as a model of human qualities. Whereas God is above the sefirot and emanates downward, we are beneath the sefirot yearning to climb upward.

The verses in First Chronicles (29:10-13) contain words and ideas which have been viewed as allusions to sefirot. These verses are part of a blessing uttered by King David, praising God as the Source of our lives. Even though our days on earth are as a shadow, they are endowed with meaning by God. In meditating the qualities of the sefirot, the questions arise: but who am I and who are my people?

1

Malkhut—Kingdom

A story is told of a Jewish community long ago and far away. A certain old man, learned and philosophical, was unable to hold down a job. Every Friday morning, he went to the rabbi to ask for charity. And each time, the rabbi gave him sufficient funds to provide for the Sabbath and the upcoming week.

But the rabbi felt uneasy about this arrangement. After all, the beggar was in fact a man of learning. Surely it was humiliating for him to have to ask for alms from the rabbi each week. The rabbi felt the poor man's pain and embarrassment.

One day, the rabbi had an idea. He would see whether a job could be created that even this beggar could hold successfully. In this way, the beggar would be able to feel that he was earning his weekly stipend rather than receiving charity. The rabbi discussed the idea with the leaders of the community. Yes, they all agreed, it would be best if the beggar could be given employment. But what could he do?

At last, a proposal was put forward that found favor in everyone's eyes. A high platform would be constructed alongside the road leading into the town and a chair would be placed on it. The beggar would be hired by the Jewish community to sit on the chair and keep his eyes on the road. His job was to keep watch for the Messiah. When he spotted the Messiah coming up the road, he was to rush into town and alert the townspeople so they could give the Messiah a proper reception.

It was agreed by the rabbi and communal leaders. And the pauper accepted the job with some satisfaction.

On the Friday morning after the first week of work, the man came to the rabbi for his pay. The rabbi paid his salary and asked him how he liked his job. "It is fine for now," said the old man.

And so the process repeated itself for several weeks.

But then came a Friday morning when, after the rabbi gave him his pay, the old man said: "Rabbi, I am quitting this job."

Astounded, the rabbi asked: "Why should you quit?"

The old man answered: "Too much pressure!"

Too much pressure? What did the old sage have in mind? His job seems to have been fairly simple and straightforward, not particularly taxing or stressful.

And yet, if we think carefully about his situation, we will realize that in fact his responsibility entailed a very stressful conflict. On the one hand, waiting for the Messiah requires infinite patience. We have been awaiting his arrival for centuries, millennia. Perhaps he will not appear for many years to come, maybe not in our lifetimes. But we wait. With infinite patience and calm confidence, we wait for the promised day when the Messiah will arrive, when peace will fill the earth, when the people of Israel will be truly free and unpersecuted. If he does not come today, perhaps tomorrow; and if not tomorrow, perhaps next week; and if not next week, maybe next year, or a few years from now, or many years from now. We are patient. We will wait.

On the other hand, waiting for the Messiah also demands an opposite attitude: infinite impatience. We don't want to wait years and centuries for the world to be rid of war, hatred, violence, injustice. We can't bear the delay. We want redemption now, as quickly as possible. We have no patience for the evil in our society and our world. We want Messiah now. We are infinitely impatient. We have waited long enough, more than long enough.

And so the old man's conflict became an unbearable source of pressure. He was the one designated to look up the road in hopeful anticipation of the coming of the Messiah. He was the one who had to spend minute after minute, day after day, always focused on the absence of the Messiah. Infinite patience was required; but he was also infinitely impatient. He could not stand the inner conflict. He quit.

To a large extent, a rabbi (and any religious Jew for that matter) can identify with the plight of the old man. We have profound faith that the Messiah will come one day, and even if he tarries we will wait for him and long for him each day. We have a vivid vision of what the world will be in the future—a world of righteousness and justice, peace and dignity, a world in which Jews can live without fear of oppression. But our vision is so powerful, we want it to be realized immediately. Every day that passes without redemption is a day lost forever.

Gershom Scholem, the great 20th century scholar of kabbalah, once described a mystic as someone who struggles with all his might against a world with which he wants more than anything to be at peace. The mystic, according to this description, is one who is infinitely impatient to realize God's kingdom on earth. He is at odds with the spiritual imperfections of this world; he yearns with all his heart for *tikkun*, correction of the universe to reflect the spiritual perfection that God has promised. He fights against this world, he is alienated from it, he focuses on the true, perfect world of spirit. He wants to be at peace, but he cannot make peace with imperfection.

On the other side of the spectrum from the mystic is the fatalist, possessed of infinite patience. Whatever is, is a manifestation of God's will. The fatalist's philosophy is clear: accept things as they are. Know your place. Develop a piety which is equated with passive quietism. Everything that happens is for the best, is part of God's plan. The fatalist is at peace with a world with which he should be at war.

But for those of us who are not fully mystics or fatalists, our struggle is to balance the claims of infinite impatience and infinite patience. We are not at peace with ourselves, and we are not at peace with the world; and yet we must constantly strive to achieve internal and external peace.

In an essay I wrote (originally published in *Moment Magazine*, September 1980), I stated:

> A religious person devotes his life to ideals, values, and observances which generally are at odds with the society in which he lives. He fights with all his power to resist succumbing to the overwhelming non-religious forces around him. Yet, he does not *want* to live his life as

a struggle. He wants to be at peace. He wants to be able to relax his guard, not always to feel under siege.

It is no simple matter to balance the inner dialectic between infinite patience and infinite impatience, between a sense of being at war with the world and desperately striving to be at peace. But a rabbi has an even greater challenge. In describing the dilemma of the modern Orthodox rabbi (in the above-mentioned essay), I wrote:

> And in the most confusing situation of all we have the enlightened Orthodox rabbi. Not only is he busy with his own personal struggles, fighting his own wars, but he also is responsible for the struggles and battles of his community. Sometimes, his congregation may not even realize there is a war. Sometimes, he may appear to be a modern version of Don Quixote. Sometimes, he is perceived as being too religious and idealistic, and sometimes, he is perceived as being crass, materialistic, secularist. For some people he is not modern enough, while for others he is a traitor to tradition.

During my first few years as rabbi, I studied Talmud with Rabbi Meyer Simcha Feldblum, then professor of talmudic literature in the Bernard Revel Graduate School of Yeshiva University. I went to his apartment in Washington Heights (New York City) several mornings a week, and we studied a variety of talmudic texts. Rabbi Feldblum, who later moved to Israel to teach talmudic literature at Bar Ilan University, was one of the great influences on my rabbinic life. He taught his students to evaluate each text in its proper historical and literary contexts. His enthusiasm for Talmud and his intellectual integrity were sources of inspiration.

At one of our sessions (in the spring of 1971), I confided in him that I was thinking of leaving the rabbinate. I had only been serving for a few years, but I found the pressures unbearable. I was not bothered by the actual rabbinic responsibilities; I was quite happy with my work and the people of the congregation. So what was my complaint? The task was too great. I had in my mind a vision of what a congregation should be in a perfect world. I thought that if I devoted myself selflessly to achieving these ideals, I would succeed in realizing my vision. But I had worked day and night, drawn on all my intellect and talent, and nevertheless nothing much was changing. The congregation was no nearer my ideal of perfection; my work was in vain; perhaps I was simply inadequate to the challenge.

Dr. Feldblum offered me a rabbinic lesson. In the days of the Holy Temples in Jerusalem, the Temple ritual required the offering of incense. The priest put together the various spices and ground them into a very fine mixture. The Talmud states that when the priest was grinding the spices, someone stood alongside him and said: "Grind it very fine, very fine grind it." Why was this person obligated to say this? The Talmud explains: "Because the voice is good for [grinding] spices." Dr. Feldblum asked: "In what way is the voice good for the grinding of spices? How does this help in the preparation of the incense?" The answer: When the priest is grinding the spices, he reaches a point where he feels his work is useless. Nothing is happening. The continued grinding makes no difference. So a person stands alongside him and tells him: keep grinding, something is happening even if you don't readily perceive it. Stay with the task until it is done properly.

"So it is," said Dr. Feldblum, "with the work of a rabbi or teacher. You work very hard, grinding away at your labors, sometimes feeling that nothing is happening, nothing is changing. Someone needs to stand up and tell you: your work is not in vain. It may seem tedious and unproductive. But keep your eye on your goal. Have patience. Keep grinding." Dr. Feldblum's voice gave me the encouragement I needed at that moment. His was the voice that said: keep grinding.

But the pressure was not to disappear. A rabbi does not simply want to grow spiritually, he wants his community to grow spiritually as well. He sees many virtues in his congregation; but he also sees failings, lack of knowledge in many religious areas, carelessness in matters of religious observance. He realizes that for many people, religion is not the top priority in their lives; for some, it is more in the realm of an old habit or superstition. But the rabbi is driven to inspire, teach, transform lives, shake spiritual apathy.

A young rabbi thinks (at least I did) that people are only too happy to deepen their religious knowledge and observance if only they are inspired to do so. The task is to find the right medium of communication, but once people hear the rabbi's message properly, they will surely see the truth of what he is teaching. But more often than not, people do not transform their lives right away. They may never transform them. They have their own thoughts and issues and concerns. They may not ever be receptive to the message of even the most talented and dedicated rabbi.

But the rabbi must grind on. If I did not succeed with this set of sermons, maybe my next sermons will break through to them. If my classes did not attract too many students this time, maybe next time I will generate greater interest. If I have not moved people to greater religious commitments through friendship, or personal example, or helping them at difficult times—then maybe I will find other ways in the future. I have to be infinitely patient. People move at their own pace and with their own rhythm, not mine.

Yes. But it is not easy to be infinitely patient, to take failure after failure and still retain confidence that the future will be better. A rabbi is, after all, also infinitely impatient.

I was fortunate in being able to discuss my frustrations with the president of our congregation, Edgar J. Nathan 3rd, and with the chairman of the ministerial committee (a sort of steering committee for the Board of Trustees), Ronald P. Stanton. Both of these men have been the best possible friends a rabbi could have. Although rabbis may not naturally feel comfortable confiding in synagogue leaders, I found such integrity and wisdom in Edgar and Ronald that I felt I could trust them with my thoughts. And I have never been disappointed in this trust.

In 1978, I had reached another serious crisis in my career as rabbi. I was in my tenth year of the rabbinate, no longer a novice. Although I had done many fine things and established many wonderful friendships in the congregation, I still felt a vast gap between ideals and reality. I was impatient to the breaking point. Edgar and Ronald advised: give yourself more time, focus on the positive changes that have occurred in the life of the congregation and in the congregants, take a long view of things. I knew they were right, and yet I felt distinctly unsatisfied as rabbi. Perhaps I was not adequately talented, creative, wise; perhaps someone else could be more successful than I in advancing the spiritual life of the congregation.

Edgar and Ronald suggested that we meet with Dr. Norman Lamm, the president of Yeshiva University, and a good friend and guide. Dr. Lamm asked me in advance of our meeting to explain exactly what was troubling me.

If I had to explain what I had accomplished as a rabbi, I could offer a fine resume. I was serving one of the great congregations of American Jewry; I was generally well liked and appreciated; I was earning a decent living; I was active in important communal organizations and projects; I had authored a number of articles and a book. What was I? A successful rabbi.

But who was I as a rabbi? To this question, which probed to my inner feelings, my answer was more complex. Yes, I was studying and teaching Torah, doing acts of charity and lovingkindness. I was in a context that allowed me to grow spiritually and to help others in their confrontations with life. But I was eminently aware of failure: I had not achieved the goals I had hoped to achieve; I no longer was certain that I ever would or could. The ideals that animated my inner life were far from realization in the real world. The thought grew within me that I could wend my way through life in my present position, giving all appearances of success and happiness; and yet be a failure in my own eyes. To me this was intolerable. I had no intention of living a lie, of betraying my ideals, of making peace with the status quo. And yet, I could see no way of accomplishing what I hoped to accomplish. My inner dynamic had tilted again to the side of impatience.

I conveyed these thoughts to Dr. Lamm, and then the four of us had our meeting. I reviewed my dilemma for them. After some discussion among all of us, Dr. Lamm made an observation. Of course you are frustrated as a rabbi. Of course your ideals are beyond your ability to bring them into full realization. That is the nature of being a rabbi, an idealistic human being. If you did not have these feelings of frustration and self-doubt, you shouldn't be a rabbi. Who was the greatest rabbi of all time? Moses! And didn't Moses have his hands full? And didn't he contend with all the spiritual failings of his people, and carry the burden of leadership with pain? Didn't he have moments when he felt he was inadequate to fulfill his mission? And didn't he fail to enter the Promised Land?

That is the nature of rabbinic leadership, said Dr. Lamm. You try to bring the world closer to spiritual perfection, knowing all along that you will not and cannot fully succeed in your efforts. You invest your life, day by day, person by person, family by family. You will help some people enrich their lives Jewishly; and some people you will fail to reach with your message. Stop worrying about your internal conflicts, and put yourself to work with greater energy and enthusiasm.

And this conversation restored my infinite patience and put it back into balance with my infinite impatience. So I did not quit.

In my years of service as a rabbi, I have had the opportunity to work with many other rabbis in many different contexts. I have served as president of the Rabbinical Council of America, the Rabbinic Alumni of the Rabbi Isaac Elchanan Theological Seminary of Yeshiva University, and the Commission on Synagogue Relations of the Federation of Jewish Philanthropies of New York. I have served as chairman of the national rabbinic cabinet of the Jewish National Fund, and as an officer or board member of numerous organizations, including the New York Board of Rabbis, the Union of Orthodox Jewish Congregations of America, the national rabbinic cabinet of the United Jewish Appeal, and State of Israel Bonds. I have worked with some of the best of rabbis and some of the worst. I have known some who were so infinitely impatient that they burned out. Some left the rabbinate, others tried to coast their way to retirement. I have known some rabbis who were so infinitely patient that nothing seemed to faze them. They found peace in their own inner worlds and seemed not to be perturbed by the religious shortcomings of their communities or the moral failings of society.

What is a rabbi in the eyes of the public? To some, he is a sort of guru, full of charisma and energy, telling them what to do and what to think. To others, he is a social worker, or politician, or administrator. For some, the rabbi is a religious functionary who presides at synagogue services and religious ceremonies. Some view a rabbi as a "public Jew" who represents the Jewish community to the non-Jewish world. Others think a rabbi is the spokesman for and teacher of Torah.

And indeed, some rabbis fit into each of these categories, and often into several—or most— of them. But people also need to know that the rabbi has an inner life, full of dynamism, faith, self-doubt, anxiety. Any rabbi deserving of the title is torn by the conflict of balancing infinite patience and infinite impatience. What is your rabbi? You can probably give a good resume. Who is your rabbi? You may not have really given this question serious thought.

The Kabbalah speaks of sefirot, divine emanations, that symbolically describe the attributes of God and His relationship with the world. The lowest of the sefirot is Malkhut (kingdom). It represents the domain in which the Divine Presence, the Shekhinah, is most approachable to human beings. An infinite gap separates physical mortals from the divine spirit of God; and yet God has created a framework, Malkhut, whereby humans can in some measure interact with the divine.

A rabbi, like every religious person, strives to achieve as high a level of relationship with God as possible. Through Torah study, prayer, contemplation, and observation of the natural world, a person attempts to establish a sort of intimacy with the divine, a feeling that God is hovering nearby, that the Shekhinah's presence can be sensed at the core of one's being.

The realm of Malkhut beckons us to strive toward the Godly. The deeper our inner religious life, the more we may experience the majesty of God; and the more we wish to do our share to establish the kingdom of God on earth.

We find ourselves participating in the image of our forefather Jacob's dream: we live on a ladder whose feet are on the ground and whose head is in heaven. And we, like the angels on Jacob's ladder, find ourselves ascending and descending. The religious life is characterized by inner movement, dialectical tensions; it is not static and fixed.

When a person gives up the spiritual struggle, a fire goes out within him. When a rabbi gives up the spiritual struggle, he becomes the persona of a rabbi, not a genuine rabbi. He ceases to be an authentic religious figure; he can only pretend to be a rabbi. A rabbi's greatest nightmare is that he will lose his inner light, becoming a caricature of a rabbi. A rabbi's greatest dream is that he will always be worthy of the rabbinic challenge. He prays that he will always be infinitely patient and infinitely impatient: and not quit.

Malkhut — Kingdom

In 1985, Rabbi Isaac Trainin, then director of the Department of Religious Affairs of the Federation of Jewish Philanthropies in New York, was putting together another volume of his "communal diary." As I had worked closely with him for some years, he asked me to contribute a short essay to his new volume on the topic: "Experiences of a Rabbi."

The following is an excerpt of that essay, which is as expressive now as it was when I wrote it fifteen years ago.

> To be a good rabbi, one needs the optimism of youth and the wisdom of age. It is difficult to combine both of these qualities. In the early stages of one's career, optimism tends to be the stronger force. As one gains years of experience, a more tranquil wisdom sets in.
>
> A rabbi becomes "old" more quickly than the average person. Rabbis are constantly involved in crisis situations. They regularly deal with death, and with birth, and with marriage, and with divorce. They share the sorrows and joys of an entire community. A rabbi may officiate at a funeral in the morning, rush back to the synagogue to perform a wedding, then attend a celebration naming a newborn baby, followed by a visit to a house of mourning. One of the challenges of the rabbinate which I learned from my earliest days is the rapid changes of emotion during relatively short spans of time, even a single day. Somehow, people expect that a rabbi can switch his emotions on or off, according to the need of the occasion. But a rabbi is only human, and has feelings of his own.
>
> Since the rabbi is intensely involved with life and death, he gains the wisdom of experience in a compressed amount of time. But this relatively quick metamorphosis has problems of its own.

A young rabbi expects that he will be able to change the world. He is filled with dreams and aspirations, and is optimistic of his ability to succeed dramatically. Experience often dampens youthful enthusiasm. It teaches one to have more realistic expectations, to accept the limitations of others and—more importantly—the limitations of one's self. But if one loses his optimism, his belief that he can indeed change the world, then it is difficult for him to be a good rabbi. He simply becomes a polite administrator, master of ceremonies, entertainer, etc. He is content to take his salary, keep the boat from rocking too much, and hold off until retirement.

A rabbi is not an endless source of knowledge and wisdom. A rabbi must always study, replenish his knowledge, renew his intellectual and spiritual content. Our sages were right in equating the study of Torah with freedom.

One of the great modern rabbis, upon his retirement, was asked what he felt was his greatest accomplishment in the rabbinate. He answered: my wife and I succeeded in raising our children to be religious Jews. Ultimately, I suppose this is the greatest accomplishment which any Jew can attain. One's first responsibility is to his own family. A good family is certainly a source of strength and encouragement to anybody, certainly a rabbi. In this regard, I have been particularly blessed with my wife Gilda and our children, Hayyim, Ronda, and Elana.

The rabbinate makes one grow "old" relatively quickly. But it also keeps one "young" and optimistic. There is always something more to be done, another challenge, another opportunity. We are still far, far away from the Promised Land. But every day, we work to move a little bit closer.

2

Netsah—Endurance

For whom does a rabbi work? On the most obvious level, he works for his congregation. The congregation employs him, pays him, and has the power to let him go. His essential obligation, thus, would seem to be to his congregation.

On a basic level, this is true. The rabbi seems to be simply an employee who is engaged and dismissed at the will of the congregation, and who is assigned certain responsibilities which he is expected to perform to the congregation's satisfaction.

On a deeper level, though, the rabbi works for the Jewish people as a whole. He is an agent of Kenesset Yisrael, the congregation of the entire people of Israel. Every individual congregation is an element in the overall peoplehood of Israel; and every synagogue, in a sense, is an "embassy" of the Jewish people. The rabbi works at the embassy, but is answerable not merely to the embassy authorities, but to the nation he represents: Kenesset Yisrael.

Rabbi Joseph B. Soloveitchik described the unique character of the Jewish people in his essay "Community" (*Tradition*, spring 1978):

> The community in Judaism is not a functional-utilitarian, but an ontological one. The community is not just an assembly of people who work together for their mutual benefit, but a metaphysical entity, an individuality, I might say, a living whole. In particular, Judaism has stressed the wholeness and the unity of Kenesset Israel, the Jewish community. The latter is not a conglomerate. It is an autonomous entity, endowed with a life of its own.

In another essay, "Repentance," Rabbi Soloveitchik made the following observation:

> The Jew who believes in Kenesset Israel is the Jew who lives with Kenesset Israel where she may be and is prepared to die for her, who hurts with her pain and rejoices in her joy, who fights her wars, suffers in her defeats, and celebrates her victories. The Jew who believes in Kenesset Israel is the Jew who joins himself as an indestructible link not only to the Jewish people of this generation but to Kenesset Israel of all generations. How? Through Torah, which is and creates the continuity of all the generations of Israel for all time.

Every Jew who lives life as a full participant in Kenesset Yisrael is part of what Rabbi Soloveitchik calls the Masorah community, the community of tradition that maintains and transmits the eternal teachings of Torah. The Masorah community is composed of all the Jews, in every generation, who devote their lives to Judaism, making every sacrifice and withstanding every danger to perpetuate the Torah way of life. Members of the Masorah community, past and present, have done something that no other people in human history has even vaguely accomplished: they have maintained an unbroken religious tradition for thousands of years, even while scattered in many lands, even in persecution, even in freedom.

The accomplishment of the Masorah community is a human phenomenon of the highest significance. It demonstrates the heroic, unflinching, enduring courage of the Jewish people. We received the Torah at Mount Sinai well over three thousand years ago. We have lived by the ideals and commandments of the Torah, and we have shared our religious insights with the world.

Not that the world has shown us much gratitude or appreciation! Although so many nations have drawn so much positive wisdom from the Hebrew Bible and traditions, they have—as a whole—given the Jewish people a very difficult time. Jewish history in Christian and Muslim lands is filled with anti-Jewish legislation, persecution, humiliation, oppression, and forced conversion. The Christian world has used, and continues to use, missionaries, including apostate Jews, to proselytize the Jews. Anti-Semitism continues to be an ugly force in the world, even in the free and democratic societies. Kenesset Yisrael, with her many tears and sufferings, has proven her power to endure with glory and tenacity. No force on earth—neither expulsions, pogroms, nor the Holocaust—has been able to destroy the people and faith of Israel. Empires and individuals that tried to destroy the Jewish people have themselves perished; and the people of Israel remains. The day will surely come, may it be soon, when the people of the world will see Kenesset Yisrael in all her heroism and grandeur, when they will stand in awe of what the Jewish people has achieved, when they will at last say to Kenesset Yisrael: thank you for all you have given to the world; thank you for the unparalleled example of faith which you have set under the most trying conditions.

A rabbi sees himself as an "employee" of Kenesset Yisrael. He represents Kenesset Yisrael in everything he does. He fights for her honor, he sacrifices for her survival, he loses sleep worrying about her future. He has accepted upon himself the obligation of strengthening and expanding the Masorah community of his generation. His work in his congregation is a contribution to the overall health of Kenesset Yisrael. It is his commitment to the Jewish people of generations past, present, and future. He invests his life in Kenesset Yisrael.

The modern-day rabbi is in many ways more fortunate than his predecessors of previous generations. We are not confronted with state- or church-sanctioned anti-Semitism, as they often were. We live at a time when a sovereign Jewish State of Israel exists and thrives, something that was lacking for nearly nineteen hundred years before Israel was reestablished in 1948. Our communities are, by and large, better off educationally, economically, politically. We have better and quicker means of communication, and can reach larger audiences through publications, radio and television, the Internet.

But our predecessors had significant advantages over us. Until the past two hundred years or so, almost all Jews felt that their identities were connected to Kenesset Yisrael. Their lives were lived within the framework of Jewish law and tradition; and even if they veered from some of the strictures and beliefs of Judaism, they knew that they were Jews in their own eyes and in the eyes of their non-Jewish neighbors and rulers. But with the era of political emancipation of Jews in the Western world, the situation of the Jewish people has changed dramatically. Jews—who for so many centuries had been deprived of civil rights and kept out of schools, government, and professions—now had more doors opened to them. While many continued to maintain their allegiance to Torah and Kenesset Yisrael, many others were eager to enter the mainstream of Western life, even if that meant watering down or surrendering their traditional Jewish way of life. New religious movements emerged among European and American Jews in order to "modernize" Judaism and make it more palatable to modernizing Jews. Increasing numbers of Jews were finding their identities outside the framework of traditional Jewish law, custom, and faith. Jews could now identify as nationalist Jews, non-Orthodox Jews, secular Jews—or they could sever their ties to Judaism altogether.

Kenesset Yisrael, which for millennia had held together the Jewish people, saw hundreds and thousands of her children voluntarily leaving her loving arms. The Masorah community became smaller and smaller. Instead of being made up of most Jews, it now was the preserve of a minority of Jews. And this minority, this remnant of Kenesset Yisrael, became increasingly fearful of the assimilation that had overcome so many fellow Jews. Some decided that survival could only be maintained by isolating themselves from the erosive qualities of mainstream society. They eschewed secular education. They ceded more authority to their rabbis and teachers. They insulated themselves and isolated themselves as much as they could. Their hope was to be able to pass on the Torah traditions to their children and future generations, so that at least their own inner group would remain loyal to Kenesset Yisrael. They saw themselves as the last bastion of authentic Torah tradition, the last fortress of the eternal Masorah community. They wanted to maintain the continuity of Jewish tradition for themselves and future generations. Some day, when all the other Jews were at last ready to return to Kenesset Yisrael, these insulated communities would be there to welcome their returning brothers and sisters.

Other traditionalists, often termed modern Orthodox or neo-Orthodox, believed it was possible to retain full loyalty to Kenesset Yisrael while at the same time participating successfully in society at large. Isolationism was criticized as a form of fearful escapism. It assumed that the Torah way of life could not survive the challenges of modernity. The modern Orthodox argued that the Torah traditions were able to stand up to every situation, every culture, every challenge—and emerge successfully. No doubt, confrontation with modernity was daunting. But so were the confrontations of the Masorah community with Hellenism and so many other isms throughout the centuries; and the Masorah community had always survived with dignity and courage.

The modern Orthodox position is not an accommodation to modernity, but a principled approach to Jewish law and tradition. It contends that Judaism's true expression has always been modern, in the sense that the rabbis of every generation have always taught Torah in relation to the society and time in which they live. While rooting themselves in the eternal truths and texts of Jewish tradition, they always had to apply ancient traditions to modern realities.

I described aspects of the modern Orthodox approach in an article published by the Rabbinical Council of America in 1985 ("Modern Orthodoxy and Halakhah: An Enquiry," *Journal of Jewish Thought*):

> The characteristic of modern Orthodoxy is that it is *modern*, that it is correlated to the contemporary world-time. Being part of contemporary world-time, it draws on the teachings of modern scholarship, it is open to modern philosophy and literature, and it relates Jewish law to contemporary world realities.
>
> A modern Orthodox rabbi does not wish to think like a medieval rabbi, even though he wishes to fully understand what the medieval rabbi wrote and believed. The modern Orthodox halakhist wishes to draw on the wisdom of the past, not to be part of the past.
>
> There is no sense in forcing ourselves into an earlier world-time in order to mold our ways of thinking into harmony with modes of thought of sages who lived several hundred or even several thousand years ago.
>
> Modern Orthodoxy requires us to live in the present world-time, knowing full well that many of the notions which we consider true and basic may become discredited in future centuries. We do not want those future generations of rabbis to be limited in their thinking to what we are thinking and teaching today. Our time is now, and only now. The Torah, which is eternal, requires Jews to go to the judge living and serving their own time.

To me, modern Orthodoxy represents the Masorah community at its best. While the non-Orthodox movements have forsaken or diluted their allegiance to the divine nature of Torah and halakhah, modern Orthodoxy has remained staunchly faithful. The Torah is God's word to the Jewish people—and to the world. The halakhah is a divinely authorized system of law and is the authentic expression of Jewish religiosity. The Torah and halakhah are living links from generation to generation. To sever Judaism from these sources is to be unfaithful to the historic Masorah community.

On the other hand, while the right-wing Orthodox are certainly faithful to the Masorah community, they are—it seems to me—abdicating their responsibility to the entire Kenesset Yisrael of this generation. They essentially operate from a self-contained spiritual fortress. In the process, they are prone to fundamentalism, obscurantism, authoritarianism. They are afraid to run the risk of living in an open and free society, feeling that they will lose too much. The modern Orthodox, while certainly aware of the spiritual risks of living as part of the modern world, are bold enough to confront the challenges directly. The modern Orthodox are concerned by the erosive forces of modern society; but are too confident and brave to run into hiding and isolation. The Torah tradition is strong enough and great enough to emerge successfully from encounters with any culture or civilization. Indeed, the Jewish people throughout history have confronted and learned from numerous civilizations. Jewish thought has benefited from the interaction with other cultures.

Modern Orthodox institutions, such as Yeshiva University, the Union of Orthodox Jewish Congregations of America, the Rabbinical Council of America, Amit Women, Emunah Women, and the Religious Zionists of America, have historically been the organizational bases of American modern Orthodoxy. They continue to be so, in spite of the growing internal pressures of religious extremism, fundamentalism, and isolationism.

In the kabbalistic scheme of sefirot, the quality of Netsah (endurance, eternity) is on the level just above Malkhut (kingdom). The task of the Masorah community is to perpetuate a rich and vital Jewish life, steeped in Torah learning and observance. This commitment can be met only by an all-encompassing concern for the spiritual and physical welfare of the entire Jewish people. A rabbi's total existence is dedicated to the endurance of Jews and Judaism.

Many rabbis, including me, serve congregations composed of Jews with different levels of Jewish learning and religious observance. Our congregation, Congregation Shearith Israel (the historic Spanish and Portuguese Synagogue of New York City, founded in 1654) is affiliated with the Orthodox movement, but members of the congregation span a spectrum of Jewish religious identification. We have no members who are right-wing religious zealots, and we have no members who are atheistic secularists. But between these extremes, we do have a considerable spread of religious ideology and commitment. Why do people who are not religious in an Orthodox sense belong to an Orthodox congregation? There are many reasons: a vestigial respect for tradition, proximity to the synagogue building, appreciation of the synagogue's decorous services, connection with Sephardic heritage, respect for the long-standing participation in American life, benefit from the wide range of educational, cultural, and social services. Some people even join because they appreciate the rabbis!

In such a diverse setting, the rabbi must be focused on maintaining a harmonious congregation and helping congregants to grow in their Jewishness—all of them on their own individual levels. This requires more energy, intelligence, compassion, and creativity than any one person can have. And yet, the rabbi must try to do his best; this is his ultimate commitment to his congregation and to Kenesset Yisrael.

How is this commitment manifested? Through words and deeds.

Words: the rabbi is first and foremost a Torah teacher, who must use all his skills and insights to convey Torah to his congregation and community. In order to teach, a rabbi must devote considerable time to study: without studying, the rabbi runs out of fuel, he has to keep recycling old ideas and lessons, he grows stale. Ultimately, he recognizes his own shallowness and loses confidence in himself as a rabbinical teacher.

Regardless of the significant time pressures on him, a rabbi must find time for Torah study each day. Study is not a luxury that may be pursued in spare time; it is the essence of a rabbi's being. If a rabbi loses his footing in Torah study, he not only undermines his authority as a rabbi, but he does a disservice to his congregation and to Kenesset Yisrael.

My experience as rabbi, which I believe is typical of most rabbis, is that I have been involved in teaching children in our synagogue religious school, working with teenagers and college students, teaching adult education to men and women. A rabbi tries to teach each group on its level; the goal is to communicate content, but also the ineffable emotion and faith that underlie the content. Sometimes the rabbi feels that he is being successful, and very often he feels that he is failing.

The modern rabbi has much competition for the attention and allegiance of his fellow Jews, most of whom do not share his singular commitment to Torah study and observance. While a growing number of parents enroll their children in Jewish day schools, many others are content to enroll their children in the congregation's religious school, which has classes on Sunday mornings and one or two afternoons per week. Even this minimal commitment to Jewish education is often not taken too seriously. Parents offer numerous excuses justifying their children's absence from religious school classes: soccer, baseball, football, basketball practice, ballet lessons, piano lessons, after-school programs, swim team. They must miss class on Sundays because the family goes away on weekends to their country home, or goes away for weekend ski trips. For many parents and children, Jewish education is at the bottom of the priority list.

An incredible feature of American Jewish life is the Bar and Bat Mitzvah observance among minimally committed Jews. The youngsters prepare their portions, participate in the synagogue ceremony, have a party to celebrate the occasion. And then, parents and children feel they have met their responsibility as Jews. More often than not, children drop out of the religious school once they have observed their Bar or Bat Mitzvah. No matter what programs and classes are offered to them, few continue with their Jewish educations past age thirteen.

Here is a typical conversation between a rabbi and the parents of a Bar or Bat Mitzvah child who had been attending the religious school.

Rabbi: Of course, you will want your child to continue with Jewish education.

Parent: Well, actually he/she doesn't want to continue. He/she now has more work in "regular" school, and needs more time for school work, sports activities, social life.

Rabbi: But it is important that the child continue with Jewish studies too.

Parent: You're right. But he/she doesn't really want to continue with religious school.

Rabbi: If your child told you that he/she didn't want to continue with math class, or science class, or English class, would you tell him/her that it was all right to drop out?

Parent: Of course not. The child is required to take those classes to get into high school and then college.

Rabbi: If you would compel your child to take classes that are for his/her ultimate good for high school and college, shouldn't you also compel him/her to grow in Jewish knowledge by attending religious classes? If you won't let him/her drop out of math class, why will you let him/her drop out of Judaism classes? Isn't the child's Jewish future of importance?

Parent: You're right. But kids have minds of their own, and I can't get him/her to continue with Jewish education. But everything will be fine. Don't worry. He/she will grow up to be a good Jew.

End of conversation. Probable end of the child's possibility of being a Jewishly educated and observant person. Likely beginning of child's alienation from Judaism.

Somehow, parents do not mind it if their children are condemned to go through life with a thirteen-year-old's Jewish education. It would not occur to them to stop their children's general education at age thirteen. Yet, they are content to raise children who are functionally illiterate Jews.

And these same parents will come to their rabbi years later to lament that their children are planning to marry out of the faith, or that they are not interested in the synagogue or Judaism, or even that they have been attracted to various cults. They somehow do not see any correlation between the way they raised and educated their children

Jewishly, and the way the children have chosen to live. If the children never were imbued with a love of Jewish learning and observance, if few sacrifices were made for the sake of a deep Jewish life, why should the grown children feel any particular loyalty to Kenesset Yisrael? They were essentially raised as non-Jews of Jewish heritage.

Some years ago, I had a conversation with an elderly member of our congregation. As he approached the end of his life, he wanted some sort of rabbinic reassurance that he had done his best as a Jew. He had been charitable, honest, kind. He had supported the synagogue and other worthy institutions. Yet, all of his four children had married out of the faith, one being a deacon in a church. His Jewish line had come to an end. He was perplexed. He could not understand how this had happened to him. I did my best to console him.

But the fact was that this man's children had received next to no Jewish education. The home in which they were raised was devoid of intense Jewish commitment; the family did not observe the laws of kashruth, did not keep the Sabbath or holidays. There were few books of Jewish content in the home. The children had attended religious school until age thirteen. They attended private schools and colleges where there were few other Jewish students, none of whom had much religious knowledge or commitment. Couldn't the parents have easily foreseen the outcome of their own actions and decisions? Couldn't they realize that they were failing in their responsibility to their own children and to Kenesset Yisrael?

In biblical tradition, the idea of eternity is conveyed by the expression *le-dor va-dor*, "from generation to generation." The Netsah (endurance, eternity) of the Jewish people is not a remote abstraction; it is demonstrated by the continuity of generations. The Masorah community has always understood this central truth and has invested its resources and energies in the religious upbringing of its children. But so many Jews today have slipped out of the Masorah community. They have put other goals before their commitment to Kenesset Yisrael. And their children have been robbed of their spiritual birthright.

Rabbi Benzion Uziel (1880–1953), late Sephardic Chief Rabbi of Israel, was alarmed at the high level of assimilation of Jews in the diaspora. Many Jewish parents felt that their children could only get ahead in life if they received a secular education by attending the "right" schools. They wanted this success even at the cost of sacrificing Jewish knowledge and observance. As Rabbi Uziel saw it, such parents argued: "We want our children to be learned doctors, writers, and merchants. We can accomplish this only in non-Jewish schools that are kind enough to allow us to enlighten and educate our sons and daughters if we only will sell our souls to them." He responded:

> Let me tell them: in all generations and in all eras and in all the places where we have been scattered, we have not lacked giants in knowledge and enlightenment. They gave honor and glory to Judaism and its Torah. The Jewish people in general stood on a higher level of worldly knowledge than all other nations; but in no place and at no time did Jews sacrifice their children to Molekh, and they did not take their education from foreign sources; rather they took the beauties of Japheth into the tents of Shem, and they learned and became enlightened in business and in general knowledge.

Jewish day schools provide a solid general education and at the same time offer religious instruction. Students who graduate from such schools are not only able to succeed in professional and business life, but are also able to maintain a rich Jewish life. But many Jewish parents in the United States still prefer to place their children in non-Jewish schools, without seeing to it that their children receive adequate religious instruction at home or in supplementary schools.

Over the years, some parents have actually approached me to complain that their children were becoming too interested in Judaism. Some felt that their children would be unable to succeed in business or the professions if they were religious. Religious observance would get in the way of their advancement. The fact that many religiously observant Jews were quite successful in business and professional life did not seem to offset their concerns. They did not want their own children being too religious, and they certainly did not want their children to make any religious demands that would upset the parents' nonreligious lifestyle.

Even when parents went along with their children's growing interest in Judaism, they sent their children to secular schools where the odds against living a religious Jewish life were high. Several of my best and most promising students in religious school eventually went off to college and ended up marrying non-Jewish spouses. A great many students have gone off to colleges where the moral and intellectual life was very far from the standards of Jewish religiosity. Due to peer pressure and a process of academic brainwashing, students feel that they should attend this college or that college: and parents either agree or don't feel they can stand in the way. That the colleges of choice might be destructive of their children's Jewish future is not the decisive factor in the decision.

A rabbi delivers sermons and lectures, engages in conversations, talks and talks about the need for absolute commitment to the Jewishness of our children and grandchildren. He reminds his congregants incessantly of the grandeur of the Masorah community, of the sacrifices needed to maintain our people from generation to generation. Fortunately, some people are influenced by his message. Unfortunately, many are not.

A rabbi's most public and ongoing podium for communication with the congregation is the synagogue pulpit. The rabbi spends a great deal of time and emotion in preparing speeches which he delivers on a regular basis to his congregants. Some congregants are in the synagogue every week, others attend less frequently, many are there only on Rosh Hashanah and Yom Kippur. No single sermon can reach everyone in the same way. In many respects, a good sermon is as good as the listener. For a sermon to work, the rabbi must have something worthwhile to say, and the congregant must be receptive to what is being said.

A great nineteenth-century sage, Rabbi Israel Salanter, observed that a sermon should be judged successful if even one person learns from or is inspired by it—even if that one person is the rabbi himself! I would add to this observation that a sermon can *only* be judged successful if the rabbi himself has learned from or been inspired by it. Few people benefit from a stale, trite, and uninspired sermon.

The success of a rabbi's sermons cannot be measured by individual sermons, but by the cumulative impact of months and years of sermons. Through sermons, a rabbi helps set the spiritual tone of a congregation. He allows the public to gain a glimpse of his inner life, to see what is important to him, to see his sensitivities, intellectual strengths—and his weaknesses. Many a time, congregants have come to me for consultation or counseling because they felt they could trust that I would understand their situation. They had gained this sense from my sermons.

From time to time, a rabbi learns that a particular sermon or set of sermons has actually changed the lives of his listeners. These are the precious satisfactions of a rabbi. He gives sermons week in and week out; but he has scant evidence that the sermons actually result in any positive dramatic changes. So when someone tells or writes the rabbi that his or her life was deeply affected by the rabbi's words, the rabbi is grateful beyond words.

I keep a file in my desk that I have named "Hang in There." When I sometimes become depressed and frustrated, I remember this file, in which I have placed special letters I have received over the years. The letters express appreciation for something I said or did that had a positive influence on the letter writer. I remember parents who decided to enroll their children in Jewish day schools, individuals who increased their level of religious observance and commitment, or who have become more charitable, more active in the synagogue, more involved in Jewish life, more committed to the well-being of the State of Israel. Surely, I have had more than enough feelings of failure and frustration; so I am all the more grateful for the feeling of having made at least a modest contribution to the ongoing eternity of Kenesset Yisrael.

When I was a rabbinical student at Yeshiva University, Rabbi Israel Miller gave a lecture to our class. He told us that when it comes to sermons, it is not so much what the rabbi says—but what the rabbi is! The most eloquent sermon is undermined if the rabbi's own character is flawed.

Preaching about kindness and justice and charity is not very effective if the rabbi himself does not personify these values in his life. Thus, a rabbi's words must be accompanied by a rabbi's deeds in establishing a religious framework for a community.

Being a public figure, a rabbi loses a certain degree of privacy. While no rabbi should tolerate a situation where he and his family feel they are living in a fishbowl observed by all, every rabbi should realize that he is a public personality. While even rabbis are entitled to private time and space, they are never totally free of their public responsibility. Anyone who wishes to live an entirely private life should not be a rabbi of a congregation. A rabbi's words and deeds are a reflection of who he is and what he represents.

At root, a rabbi is an agent of Kenesset Yisrael, striving to keep the eternal link of Jewish generations moving ever onward. The greatest satisfaction is seeing families communicate their Jewish way of life from generation to generation. It is a source of spiritual happiness to see generations of the same families in synagogue together, to witness the continuing commitments of generations to the Jewish tradition. On the other hand, it is profoundly sad to see Jewish family lines come to an end through ignorance, apathy, or lack of commitment to Kenesset Yisrael. American Jewry is experiencing a very high rate of interfaith marriage, with many Jews willingly marrying out of the Jewish tradition. In the old days, such marriages were considered shameful for the families involved; now interfaith marriages are regularly written up in the *New York Times* and other public media. Every interfaith marriage is a wound in the fabric of Kenesset Yisrael. It is possible that some of the children of such marriages will end up within the Jewish fold, but the statistics show that the overwhelming majority of children of interfaith marriages end up outside the Jewish community.

Why would so many Jews cut off themselves and the future generations of their families from the eternal Kenesset Yisrael? Why, after so many generations of Jewish forebears, would they willingly commit spiritual suicide, ending their line of the Jewish family tradition? It is demonstrated in various sociological studies that the most likely Jewish candidates for intermarriage are those who were raised with a minimal level of religious observance and commitment. Many American Jews have only tenuous ties to the teachings and practices of Judaism; they do not see it as much of a sacrifice to give up their connection to the tree of Jewish life. They give away a great treasure, because they do not even realize that they possess a treasure of incomparable value. They do not mourn their loss, because they do not understand how much they have lost. Their interfaith weddings might even have included the participation of a "rabbi"; they may have danced a Jewish dance; they may have sung a Jewish song. But every member of the Masorah community cries for each and every Jew who leaves Kenesset Yisrael. Will Kenesset Yisrael survive? Yes, there is no question of that. Kenesset Yisrael is eternal. There will always be Jews and a Jewish people. But we do not want even one Jew to give up the chance to be part of Kenesset Yisrael. It is tragic to see a Jewish line die.

I have been fortunate to have communicated and worked with many individuals who have chosen to return to Kenesset Yisrael. Some were assimilated Jews who decided they wanted to deepen their Jewish knowledge and spirituality. Others were individuals who had been raised as non-Jews, but then discovered that they had Jewish ancestry. Somehow, the voice of their Jewish ancestors called out to them; and they responded by finding their way back into the Jewish fold.

I have recently been in touch with a young man, raised as a non-Jew, whose ancestors were members of our congregation. In the course of doing a genealogical study, he discovered that he was a descendant of a prominent Jewish family. He could not understand why they had left Judaism. The more he studied, the more he was convinced that he should convert to Judaism and return to the heritage of his ancestors. In one of his letters to me, he wrote:

> While both my father's parents were Jewish, he was not raised in a religious home. My mother is not Jewish and I was not raised Jewish at all. I have been doing my family genealogy for several years now, and have come to the conclusion that I have lost something great by not being raised Jewish. The more I learn about Judaism, and especially the long line of Jews that came before me, I think it would be the ultimate in arrogance for me to ignore my place in that line.

The Jewish yearnings in the hearts and souls of those who have been far removed from Jewish religious life are a source of encouragement to the Jewish community. The eternal Kenesset Yisrael continues to draw its children back into her loving arms; we pray that the day will soon come when all the stray Jewish children will return home to their faith and their heritage.

Rabbi Haim David Halevy, late Sephardic chief rabbi of Tel Aviv, was one of the great rabbinic sages of modern times. In one of his responsa (*Asei Lekha Rav*, vol. 4, no. 8), he raised an interesting question. In describing the exodus of the ancient Israelites from Egypt, the Torah states that Pharaoh *expelled* them. Yet why would it have been necessary to expel slaves? Certainly, they would have been glad to leave on their own! The answer is offered: Although many Israelites did indeed want to leave Egypt, a large number were afraid to go. They were used to living as slaves; they feared the uncertainties of a new life in an unknown land in untried conditions. So it was necessary for them to be expelled, since they would not have left on their own. Rabbi Halevy asks: Why was it necessary for them to have been expelled? Why didn't God simply redeem those Israelites who wished to be free, and leave the others in servitude? The answer: Redemption must necessarily include all of the people, even those who are not interested in being redeemed.

Rabbi Halevy states that this model of redemption will be true for the future redemption of Israel as well, namely, it will include all Jews. It will entail the ingathering of the scattered Jewish exiles; not even one will be left behind. Even Jews who have been converted to other religions, even those who have been completely assimilated and now pass as non-Jews—all will return to the loving arms of the Jewish people. In this way, the future redemption will be a complete and permanent redemption.

Kenesset Yisrael will reclaim all her children, those of the Masorah community and those who have strayed. The Netsah (eternity) of the Jewish people will be fully established. The teachings of the Torah will flow as the waters, from generation to generation. And the world will be filled with the knowledge of God.

3

Hod—Splendor, Majesty

A story is told about a challenge made by the accusing angel one Yom Kippur night. Jews throughout the world had gathered in their synagogues to pray for forgiveness from the Almighty. They were fasting in contrition; they were pouring out their hearts seeking atonement. God, seated on His heavenly throne, was taking great pride in the piety and devotion of the Jewish people.

The accusing angel, though, could not leave well enough alone. He wanted to humiliate the Jews. He came before God and said that their prayers were not sincere. The accusing angel then produced a machine which he claimed could determine the true motivations of the Jews. He said: "Let us take all the words of their prayers and place them in this machine. The machine will squeeze the words to their essence, and then we will see what they are really after."

God agreed to the experiment.

The accusing angel gathered all the prayers and put them into the machine. Out came the words: "Money, money, money."

"Aha," said the accusing angel. "Now you see what the Jews are really praying for: money. I told you they were not sincere!"

But before God could become angry, the defending angel came forward. "Just a moment," he said. "Let us take the prayers of the Jews and put them through the machine a second time." The Almighty agreed, as the accusing angel frowned haughtily.

The defending angel took the prayers and poured them back into the machine. And out came: "Money for our synagogues, money for our yeshivot, money to help the poor and downtrodden, money to assist the needy in the land of Israel."

The accusing angel was abashed. The Almighty was content with the prayers of His children of Israel.

The wonderful ideals and traditions of Judaism find expression in a variety of institutions, all of which require proper financial backing. Those who are most involved in the idealistic side of Judaism often find themselves also involved in the practical side: fundraising.

Rabbis are not professional fundraisers and do not see themselves as such. Most are uncomfortable about asking people for money. They feel it is undignified, awkward, beneath the rabbinic calling. And just the same, most rabbis engage in fundraising at a level that even they must find astounding.

In my thirty years as a rabbi, I have been involved in raising many millions of dollars. Fundraising was never part of my official job description, and it would not have occurred to me to ask for fundraising responsibilities from our synagogue board. But in retrospect, I see that I have been regularly engaged in raising funds for one cause or another.

It is not because I wanted to raise funds or felt that I had any particular talent for this activity. It is because I have felt such an overwhelming responsibility for the well-being of Jews and Judaism. Indeed, all Jews who see themselves as members of the Masorah community cannot help but be fundraisers. If we want Jewish life to flourish, we have to have the money to sustain it. We pray for money so that we will have proper synagogues and schools, so that the State of Israel will be strengthened, so that the hungry will be fed and the ill be treated. If we believe in a cause, we support it by our own giving and by calling on others to do their share.

The Kabbalah teaches that two tendencies operate in the world: the power of receiving and the power of giving. The power of receiving is characteristic of all worldly creatures; all receive sustenance from the Almighty. Human beings also receive assistance and support from other human beings. We could not live without receiving—from parents, spouses, teachers, friends, clients, customers, business and professional associates. We survive and thrive because we take so much from so many.

The power of giving represents the other side of the pendulum. We do not only take from others; we are obliged also to give. We provide sustenance, guidance, and assistance to others, helping them to live better lives.

The power of receiving connects humans with the animal and mineral worlds. Although necessary for our existence, it is not an expression of humanity at its loftiest. The power of giving is modeled after the ultimate Giver, God, Who gives without needing to receive anything back in return.

The more we utilize the power of giving, the more we emulate God.

If someone takes but does not give back commensurately, the Kabbalah describes him as one who has eaten the "bread of shame." He has not earned his bread; he has taken beyond what he was entitled to. He was dominated by the power of receiving rather than the power of giving. He thinks he has come out ahead, because he has received more than he has given. But in fact, he has sacrificed his human dignity to his greed. He is guilty of eating the bread of shame; he has proven himself to be an unworthy person.

The *Shulḥan Arukh*, the classic code of Jewish law, notes that one who contributes ten percent of his income to charity is considered a person of average generosity. One who contributes twenty percent is truly generous. One who contributes less than ten percent is considered miserly. The issue is not only the percentage given to charity, but the attitude of the donor. A generous person gives a sufficient portion of his income for charitable purposes, and does so with a good heart and warm spirit of kindness.

People have a fairly objective way of measuring their own generosity. Each year, we prepare our financial data for income taxes. We can see very clearly how much we have spent, on what we have spent it; how much we have given for charitable purposes. Indeed, the way we spend our money is a fairly accurate indication of our moral values; it is a clearer indication of who we are than what we may think and say about ourselves.

Some people spend a high percentage of their incomes on luxuries, and give only a small percentage to worthy causes and needy individuals. I know people who have spent many thousands of dollars on a luxury vacation, and then donated eighteen dollars to the synagogue on their safe return. Others have spent huge sums on lavish weddings for their children, and have contributed little to the synagogue or other worthy institutions. Some have contributed nothing at all, and even have delayed paying their synagogue bills so that they could cover their other wedding expenses. People who have no problem spending two hundred and more dollars for an evening of dinner and theater make minuscule contributions to UJA-Federation and other communal charity funds.

Some years ago, I heard of a person who had contributed several hundred thousand dollars to a society for the prevention of cruelty to animals. That same year, this person contributed several thousand dollars to the United Jewish Appeal. A UJA fundraiser confronted him with the question: "Is the survival of animals one hundred times more important to you than the survival of the Jewish people? Certainly, it is meritorious to support efforts to spare animals from suffering. But on the scale of one's values, shouldn't one be giving considerably more to spare human beings from suffering?" The person came to realize that the amount of money invested in particular causes was a reflection of his scale of values. The more important causes should receive more significant support.

The Ethics of the Fathers describes four attitudes toward giving. The worst type is characterized by a person who does not give and does not want others to give either. His power of giving has been suppressed by selfishness and greed; but he wants others to be as miserly as he, so that he will not look bad in their eyes. He eats the bread of shame and wants others to do likewise.

Another category is represented by the person who does not give but is happy to let others give. Such a person wants communal institutions to thrive and wants those in need of charity to receive assistance, but he does not want to give himself. Let others shoulder the burden and pay the bills. He can come up with dozens of excuses why he cannot or should not give, and why others ought to do the contributing.

A third category consists of those who give but do not wish others to give. Such individuals are happy to give, but they want to do so in a way that makes their generosity conspicuous. They give in order to gain prestige or power; they do not want competition in the field of philanthropy.

The highest category is composed of those who give and who want others to give. They recognize that the philanthropic needs are vast and that everyone needs to participate to the fullest. The goal is not merely to have properly funded institutions; it is to foster the spirit of giving and Godliness among the entire community. It is not possible to have too many charitable dollars; the needs always exceed our ability to meet them.

In his capacity as a fundraiser, albeit an unofficial one, the rabbi confronts each of these four types of individuals. I have been blessed beyond words with knowing a number of individuals in the highest category. They have generous natures; they give; they inspire others to give. They not only help maintain and develop institutions of Jewish life, but they create a communal spirit that fosters giving, sharing, building. Their commitment and enthusiasm set the example for other members of the community.

This category includes people on all financial levels. It is not a matter of dollars so much as an attitude of giving and inspiring others to participate. I have had the pleasure of working with wealthy philanthropists whose contributions have been in the millions of dollars. Likewise, I have had the pleasure of dealing with individuals of more modest means, but who have given proportionately large sums.

During the 1980s and early 1990s, for example, we were involved in raising funds for the United Jewish Appeal–Federation of Jewish Philanthropies of New York, in order to help in the rescue and resettlement of Jews from the former Soviet Union and Ethiopia. Thousands of Jews were being brought to Israel, and the costs involved were staggering. Our congregation, along with so many other congregations, raised funds to assist in this life-saving work. A number of wealthy individuals made sizable contributions. But many people of more modest means made contributions that, if not as large in dollar terms, were very large in the spirit of giving. One congregant did not have enough cash available to make the gift he felt was warranted, so he took out a commercial loan (with interest) and contributed the amount he thought he could manage on this basis. I told him: "You are not obligated to go into debt to give charity." He answered: "If my life were at stake, as are the lives of the Russian and Ethiopian Jews, I would want other Jews to sacrifice to save me. I am only doing what is right. Lives are on the line."

But in another campaign on behalf of Ethiopian Jews, I faced a person of a different category. He sent me a letter expressing his deep concern for the plight of the Jews of Ethiopia, urging that our congregation take a leadership role in offering assistance. At the time, I was on the board of the American Association for Ethiopian Jews. Delighted with this expression of support, I thanked this individual for his interest and asked if he would be willing to host a parlor meeting in his home to raise funds for the rescue of Ethiopian Jews. He begged off. I asked him if he would make a personal contribution to the cause. He told me he would think about it. He must still be thinking about it, since he never sent in a check. He was one of those who do not themselves give, but want others to do so. Such people feel they have done enough to support a worthy cause if they simply express a pious sentiment.

In other situations, I have come across individuals who were willing to contribute, quietly and anonymously, but were absolutely unwilling to solicit contributions from others. They were content to do their own giving, but did not feel the motivation or inner urgency to bring others into the circle of givers.

In a few cases, I have known individuals of the worst category: people who would not contribute and who wanted no one else to contribute either. They complained about the real or imagined inefficiencies and errors of the charitable institutions. Not only would they offer no support, they told others not to give. One such person complained to me about the campaign on behalf of Soviet and Ethiopian Jews; he made numerous charges against Israel, UJA-Federation, organizations working with and on behalf of Soviet and Ethiopian Jews. He could not find one virtue in all the people and agencies that were working so selflessly to help save Jewish lives. After listening to his foolish diatribe for several minutes, I asked him: "Please tell me the name of any charitable agency which you think is worthy of support. We will have a campaign for its benefit and you can be chairman." He sidled away, and never came back to me with his complaints. But he did not stop complaining to others, seeking to discourage their participation in charitable, humanitarian efforts. Such a person eats the bread of shame every day of his life, and yet thinks of himself as a fine person!

In the mid-1980s, I had ongoing correspondence with a person who also fit into the worst category. He was critical about the Jewish establishment, the State of Israel, everything connected with organized Jewish life. He not only did not contribute time, money, or energy to try to be helpful in any way; he constantly offered criticisms filled with bitterness and anger. I tried a variety of approaches to try to steer him onto a better course, but everything failed. Finally, I lost patience with him. The following is an excerpt from a letter I wrote him on August 7, 1985.
(I think its message can be readily applied to others like him):

> In my sixteen years working in the rabbinate, I have learned that people who constantly express disappointment in the "establishment," or in "Jewish leadership," or in the State of Israel, are generally very frustrated people who are really most disappointed in themselves. They feel unneeded, unwanted; their egos are bruised because no one pays them the attention they feel they deserve. So they vent their hostility on a few general targets as a way of making themselves feel important, at least in their own eyes.
>
> Every intelligent person should have his eyes open. He should realize that there are good things and bad things about every person, every society, every country. He must be troubled by the faults and encouraged by the good things. He needs to keep balance. To offer constant praise is the sign of a fool. To offer constant criticism is the sign of a fearful and frustrated person.
>
> I have written and lectured extensively about social problems in Israel. I have spent time living in a slum area in Tel Aviv. I have never hesitated to express my opinion,

both in praise and in criticism, of the social, political, and spiritual condition of Israel and the entire Jewish people. But I believe in building, not in destroying. I have led our Congregation to assume a major financial obligation in the Project Renewal Program (providing funds to help slum areas in Israel).

Every Jew who has a real sense of Jewish destiny will want to do his share to make things better. Neither you nor I can afford to wait until the Messiah comes to save the situation miraculously. We must work constructively and tirelessly to strengthen the first Jewish commonwealth in nearly nineteen hundred years. Each Jew can either choose to be part of the process, or to stand on the sidelines and watch. The future is with those who are part of the enterprise. The critics on the sidelines nod their heads watching, while others participate in the excitement of nation-building.

People who do not participate constructively to the best of their ability deprive themselves of a share in community building. They are viewed by others as unpleasant hangers on. And deep down, they view themselves as failures.

As I write this book, our congregation is in the midst of a major capital and endowment campaign. We are raising funds to repair and restore our landmark synagogue building, which was originally dedicated in May 1897. We are seeking to bolster our endowment funds so that we can better serve our congregation and community: youth work, educational programs, social action, cultural and historical projects, nursery and religious schools, outreach work, publications, and so forth. The campaign has taken much of my time and energy, even though we have a wonderful committee and fundraising team. Rabbis seem naturally predisposed to become actively involved in fundraising because they want communal life to be strengthened to its maximum. Moreover, it is often the rabbi alone who knows all the members of the congregation, who has been with them in good times and bad, who has taught them and their children, who has performed weddings for members of their families, who has buried their dead. Especially if a rabbi has been with the same congregation for many years, he has come to know his congregants and they have come to know him. A rabbi will attend endless meetings, dinners, parlor meetings, receptions, appeals, solicitations of funds. The goals are too important; the needs are too urgent; neither time nor effort can be spared. Each moment lost, is lost forever.

The Ethics of the Fathers teaches that if there is no flour, there is no Torah. That is, if the material basis of life is lacking, then the spiritual basis of life also suffers. However, one must always keep in mind that the material concerns are means to an end, not the end in themselves. People sometimes get so bogged down in caring for their physical needs that they spend little time developing their spiritual natures and meeting their religious needs.

A rabbinic parable tells of a poor man who was struggling to support his family. He learned of a faraway land that was filled with precious jewels. A ship would soon be leaving for this land, and it had room for him as a passenger. But the ship would only return after a long interval; so if the man chose to go to the faraway land, he would have to remain there a considerable time. His wife agreed that he should make the voyage. He would be able to obtain valuable jewels and bring them back to support his family in wealth and honor.

So the man boarded the ship and was off to make his fortune. Sure enough, the ship arrived at the faraway land, and it was indeed filled with treasures. The earth was covered with diamonds, rubies, emeralds, and all types of precious stones. He hurriedly filled his pockets with jewels; he stuffed his bags with gems. He was now an extraordinarily rich man. He rejoiced in the thought of how wealthy he and his family would be.

But in the faraway land, the man soon realized that his precious stones were without value. They were so abundant and so readily available that no one paid any attention to them. None of the storekeepers would accept them as payment for merchandise. Rather, the currency of this land was wax candles. These were hard to come by and were very highly valued by the people. Everyone strove to accumulate as many wax candles as possible; their wealth and power were measured in numbers of candles.

It did not take long for the man to recognize his need for wax candles. He worked hard to gain as many as he could. Soon, he had accumulated a large number of them. He emptied his pockets and bags of the diamonds, rubies and emeralds, and filled them with wax candles. In this new land, he became prominent and wealthy. He had heaped up a huge amount of candles.

Time passed. It was now time for the man to return to his family. The ship was ready to leave. Quickly, the man packed as many wax candles as he could, so that he could bring them back to his wife. He loaded himself with as many candles as he could carry, and proudly boarded the ship.

When he arrived home, his wife eagerly greeted him; she asked to see the treasures he had brought back. Proudly, the man opened his bags and emptied his pockets. He stacked up piles of wax candles.

His wife was astonished. "You spent all that time in the faraway land, a land filled with precious jewels, and you brought back only piles of worthless wax candles? Are you joking with me?"

Then, suddenly, the man realized he had made a terrible mistake. When he had arrived in the faraway land, he knew he was supposed to gather diamonds and emeralds and rubies; but he had soon forgotten his mission. Influenced by the economics of the land, he had come to value candles and ignore jewels. Finally, he had completely forgotten his original mission; he put all his energy into the accumulation of wax candles and thought he had been successful. But now, back home, he saw that he had lost sight of his goal. He had missed his opportunity to bring back real treasures, and instead had come back with common candles that were worth very little.

And so it is, goes the parable, with the human soul. It is sent from its spiritual home on a voyage to earth. It is told that it has the opportunity to gather the most wonderful treasures—Torah, mitzvot, spiritual experiences—and that these are available for the taking. But once it arrives on earth, it sees that these spiritual treasures are not much valued; rather, people are busy accumulating material wealth. So the person begins to forget about the spiritual treasures he is supposed to bring home with him, and instead devotes himself to gaining material wealth.

But the day comes when the soul is called to return home. It comes before the Almighty and shows what it has gained from its voyage. It empties its pockets and bags; yet all that it has gathered is of little account in the world of spirit. "But," asks the Almighty, "where are the real treasures you were sent to find? Where are your Torah and mitzvot, where are your spiritual gains, where are the genuine treasures you were supposed to return with?" And the soul is humiliated. It realizes that it had forgotten its original mission on earth. It was sidetracked by earthly economics, so that it lost sight of the real treasures it was supposed to attain. And now, after having spent a lifetime on earth, it has returned to God with worthless piles instead of with spiritual treasures. How foolish it had been!

Yes, as long as we sojourn on this earth, we need to earn and spend the currency that is deemed valuable here. But we must never forget our real mission: to enrich our spiritual treasures, to strengthen our souls, to return our souls to God filled with Torah and mitzvot, deeds of righteousness and compassion. We must never lose sight of what is temporal and what is eternal.

In the kabbalistic scheme of sefirot, the quality that is parallel to Netsah (endurance, eternity) is Hod (splendor, majesty). Human dignity cannot be attained without a highly developed power of giving. Splendor and majesty entail transcendence of self, reaching out to others and to the Almighty. One who is locked into himself and his possessions lacks an essential ingredient of human dignity. He eats the bread of shame. Unless you nourish your spirit as well as your body, you fail to attain the spiritual majesty of which human beings are capable.

In Jewish life, certain key institutions encompass the quality of Hod. They speak to our inner selves; they raise us to higher levels; they teach us to aspire beyond ourselves. They remind us of our ultimate mission on earth.

The synagogue exists as a religious center. I am fortunate in serving a congregation that has a magnificently beautiful synagogue sanctuary. Just entering the synagogue, one immediately senses its splendor and majesty. The synagogue is a sacred space: the outside world remains outside; the inner world allows us to think, to pray, to set our priorities in order. The synagogue service is conducted with exquisite grace and beauty, linking us—through the liturgy and traditions—with the generations that came before, and with the generations yet to come.

It amazes me that many Jews actually live their lives without spending considerable time in a religious sanctuary. They deprive themselves of a splendid framework for quiet prayer and introspection; they miss an extraordinary opportunity for Jewish spiritual growth.

People often complain about their synagogue: it does not give them a spiritual feeling, it is too noisy, the congregants are too concerned with social and material matters, the liturgy is not relevant, and on and on. In some cases, these criticisms may be valid. If so, they should seek another synagogue in which to worship. If no other is available, they should work with the leadership of their synagogue to improve the situation.

But often, the problems of spiritual fulfillment in a synagogue are not all—or even mainly—the fault of the synagogue service. The problems are with the congregants.

Rabbi Haim David Halevy offered the following insight. When rain falls on the earth, it provides sustenance and helps make things grow. Rain, in proper measure, is a great blessing. But the effectiveness of the rain's blessing is contingent on the nature of the field on which it falls. If the farmer has cultivated the field properly, the rain will cause an abundant crop to grow. But if the field has been left uncultivated, the rain will bring forth weeds and thistles. The rain is the same in both cases; it has the power of blessing within it. The difference is in the level of preparedness of the fields.

So it is with prayer. God's spirit, like the rain, pours over us with the power of blessing. If we are properly cultivated spiritually, we receive this blessing and it is a source of sustenance and growth for us. But if we are not spiritually cultivated, then the blessing is diminished or lost. Those who pray must develop their spiritual natures so as to be receptive to the power of prayer. To participate fully in the synagogue liturgy requires thoughtful study of the liturgy. The more one understands the service, the deeper the experience of its blessings.

The synagogue's mission is to keep the community focused on its ultimate mission in life. Through prayer, it keeps us in touch with God; it keeps us striving to transcend ourselves. Through sermons, lectures, and classes, it keeps us in touch with the teachings and values of the eternal Kenesset Yisrael; it reminds us what we must do to be faithful members of the Masorah community. Through social programs, it brings us closer together as a community. It teaches us to share our lives with others, to be of generous spirit, to avoid eating the bread of shame. The more closely we are identified with the synagogue and its message, the more meaningful our lives can be.

Aside from the synagogue, the Jewish community maintains other institutions that are vital expressions of its ideals. Jewish day schools and high schools, yeshivot, Yeshiva University—all are dedicated to teaching the tenets of Torah to the young. Some communities and synagogues have a beit midrash, a study hall, where people may gather to study on their own, or under the guidance of teachers. Synagogues devote considerable energy and resources to Torah teaching and Torah study.

Rabbi Joseph Soloveitchik, drawing on a comment in the Talmud, noted that the goal of one who studies Torah is to become "married" to the Torah. The student yearns to come closer to Torah, to study it as fully and deeply as possible. With years of profound devotion to the Torah, a student begins to feel a real sense of intimacy with it; life is seen through the words and ideals of Torah. When one's thoughts and deeds are inextricably linked to Torah, one is symbolically "married" to the Torah. Few people reach this level; but all should be striving for it.

The Jewish community maintains and supports agencies that provide assistance to the needy, the ill, the bereaved, the lonely, the psychologically troubled. These agencies are natural outgrowths of a Torah vision of life, a life that demands concern for others and an effort to alleviate suffering. Humanitarianism is an essential aspect of the religious Jewish worldview.

Along with the communal charity organizations, the synagogue also is a destination of needy individuals who seek financial assistance. People regularly turn up at the synagogue looking for handouts. Some are genuinely in need. Others are con artists who try to take advantage of the rabbi's good nature. The rabbi deals with a steady stream of people on the bottom of the economic ladder—unfortunates, misfits, derelicts—and tries his best to be of genuine assistance. Each of these individuals not only takes money from the rabbi, but also takes the rabbi's time and emotional energy.

As part of our social action program, our congregation operated a shelter for the homeless for ten years. I first suggested this project in a sermon. Later, I worked with a few activists until we were able to put the program into operation. We took in ten homeless men from Sunday through Thursday nights; the shelter generally operated from December through March. Many congregants became active volunteers in the maintenance of the shelter. It provided an opportunity for members of our congregation to be personally involved in helping those in need. It also enabled us to better appreciate the situation of so many people who find themselves homeless in America.

The Jewish community, led by synagogues, also supports institutions and agencies that are vital to a Jewish religious infrastructure: mikvahs (ritual baths), kashruth boards, eruv committees, synagogue service organizations, rabbinic organizations.

Those who live full Jewish lives are constantly striving to support and improve Jewish communal life. A rabbi's blessing is to be able to work with so many idealistic and dignified Jews who do so much for so many. A rabbi's frustration is dealing with individuals who are apathetic or ungenerous when it comes to the institutions of Jewish life. A rabbi's challenge is to keep himself and his community from eating the bread of shame. While striving to maintain the physical structures of Jewish life, we must always keep focused on the spiritual ideals and values they represent.

4

Yesod—Foundation

A story is told of a great sage who was traveling on a train somewhere in Eastern Europe. He was an elderly man with a long gray beard. He was dressed in traditional Eastern European rabbinic garb—black hat, long black coat.

A nonreligious Jew was sitting in the same car, near the rabbi. This man was clean-shaven, wore no hat, and was dressed according to the modern style. The "enlightened" Jew was annoyed by the appearance of the old sage. He challenged the rabbi: "Why are you so old-fashioned? Why can't you adapt to the modern world?"

The rabbi responded calmly: "I am modern. It is you who are old-fashioned."

"How can you say such a thing?" retorted the enlightened man.

The rabbi said: "You are very old-fashioned. You follow the ways of our ancestors of antiquity, who were idolaters. I am modern. I follow the new insights that God gave the world at Mount Sinai. Whereas you have regressed to the level of the ancient pagans, I follow the progressive ideas of the Torah."

The rabbi's retort, though made as a quip to put off his critic, contains an important insight. The terms "modern" and "old-fashioned" ought not to be evaluated exclusively by chronological criteria, but by the degree of spiritual advancement. Modern does not necessarily denote progress; old-fashioned does not necessarily imply outgrown and no longer of value.

Maimonides, in his classic code of Jewish law, points out that in ancient times men and women got together as couples based on their physical and emotional attractions. The Torah came along to change that style of life. The Torah sanctified marriage and presented specific laws to govern sexual relationships. It taught human beings that the relationship between a man and a woman should not be established solely to satisfy physical urges or sociological pressures. Holiness, purity, love, and mutual commitment were to be essential ingredients in such relationships.

The Torah tradition represented a vast step forward for humanity. It took human beings seriously—as human beings; not as animals, not as objects. It demanded more of us. It expected us to live our lives not as slaves to our desires, but as masters of ourselves. The Talmud states that slaves prefer a life without moral constraints; but free people are ready to accept the challenge of living on a higher spiritual level.

Many aspects of modernity tend to be old-fashioned, in the sense that they are a regression to pre-Torah times. Sex and violence dominate much of popular culture—movies, television, pornography, even music. The so-called new morality, where men and women engage in sexual relations without the genuine commitment of love and marriage, is actually a throwback to primitive times, as described by Maimonides.

The philosopher Martin Buber delineated three types of human relationships. The I-it relationship is when humans relate to one other as objects. Sometimes, we are not interested in a serious human interaction; we just want something done for us. We see the other person as an "it," an object that satisfies our needs and wants: selling us merchandise, giving us dinner, cutting our hair, delivering our mail, offering us gratification.

The I-thou relationship is when human beings relate to one other as human beings created in the image of God. We see in the other not someone who can do things for us, but someone who is unique and special, worthy of love and respect. While even the best human relationships involve both the I-thou and I-it aspects, it is the I-thou component that focuses on the other as a fellow subject, not as an object. When we look into the eyes of another human being and sense a warmth of understanding and empathy, we engage in the I-thou relationship. Sometimes, these are brief and fleeting moments; sometimes they endure for a lifetime. But it is precisely the I-thou relationships that make our lives worth living, that provide real happiness and meaning.

The I–Eternal Thou relationship describes the human experience of God. God is envisioned not as an It that exists merely to provide for our needs. Rather, God is felt as the ultimate Subject, the ultimate Thou. God is the source of love and wisdom; when we sense God as Thou, we feel a deep inner happiness and fulfillment.

Drawing on Buber's categories, we might say that Torah Judaism keeps us focused on the I-thou and the

I–Eternal Thou, while appreciating that I-it relationships are also part of life. Much of modern culture, in contrast, highlights the I- it. People are treated, and come to treat themselves, as objects.

A certain photographer practices his art by taking pictures of large groups of naked people. He recently planned to photograph such a group in Times Square, New York City. The city blocked his plan, objecting that the proposed shot would cause massive disruptions in a congested part of town. The photographer challenged the city in court, arguing his First Amendment right of freedom of expression. He portrayed himself as a martyr on behalf of civil liberties; what right had the city to suppress his artistic expression? While this dispute was going on, the *New York Times* printed an article in which it quoted the photographer's explanation of his artistic methods. He said that his photography sought to teach people to see naked humans as objects of art, not objects of sex. This was his justification for his artistic style.

What the photographer says he is doing is treating human beings as objects of art. But should human beings be so treated? Isn't it just as degrading to think of humans as objects of art as objects of sex? Shouldn't human beings be thought of as subjects, as dignified images of God? This photographer, who ostensibly passes as an avatar of modernity, is actually old-fashioned. He represents a pre-Torah worldview where human beings were seen as objects, things.

During the summer, we vacation in Long Beach, a lovely town on the Atlantic Ocean. We often walk on the boardwalk and have the opportunity to observe the many people who come to enjoy this resort area. It is astounding to see what people will do in order to be noticed. They have so internalized the pre-Torah values of society that they treat themselves as objects. They seem to have given up on maintaining their own spiritual dignity. People wear swim suits and sportswear that are very skimpy or tight or neon bright. They cover themselves with tattoos. They have pierced ears, noses, navels, lips. It is particularly pathetic to see middle-aged and elderly people following these fashions, as though they somehow think they still appear to be young and modern by so doing. In fact, they—even more than the younger people who seem not to know better—appear tragically ludicrous.

These tendencies are not confined to a summer beach community. They are obvious throughout society. The stated and implied message of much of American culture is: be sexy, be noticed, look young.

Dr. Norman Lamm, the president of Yeshiva University, has made the following observation: "One who lacks the sense of *kavod*, of inner dignity and worth, will expose himself, as if to say, 'look at me. Am I not beautiful? Am I not smart? Do you not like me?' The lack of *kavod* leads to exhibitionism, the opposite of *tseniut* (modesty), whereas a sense of *kavod* will normally result in the practice of modesty or *tseniut*."

The Torah tradition teaches high standards of modesty, not because it is ashamed of the human body—it is not; but because it is proud of the human soul. It fully recognizes and endorses respect for and admiration of the human body; but it places a higher premium on human dignity. When human beings treat their bodies primarily as objects of sexual attraction or art, they sacrifice their true human dignity. They revert to the old-fashioned, primitive style of life that predated the advances of Torah.

One can be modest, and still have one's own personal style. Modesty does not mean that everyone must dress and behave in exactly the same manner. Yet, the demands of modesty and self-respect create boundaries beyond which a person of dignity will not want to go.

In the kabbalistic system of sefirot, the level above Netsah and Hod is known as Yesod (foundation). The sexual impulse is related to Yesod. The sex drive, which is so powerful and can seem to be so uncontrollable, is supposed to serve as a source of foundation and stability for human life.

It is the means of human procreation, and thus serves as the basis of human continuity. It is also related to love, intimacy, total sharing of self; in this sense, it is essential for the foundation of a loving and sharing personality. On the other hand, if the sexual impulse is not controlled, it results in treating oneself and others as sexual objects. It lowers one's human dignity. It becomes the foundation for a worldview that fixates on sex and violence.

Being a rabbi means to stand up for Torah values in a society that is in many ways inimical to them. The general tenor of popular culture is old-fashioned; it is more interested in thrills than serious relationships; it fosters a spirit of sexual license rather than dignified sexual commitment, it glorifies sexuality and violence rather than modesty and long-term work to improve human relationships.

Teaching Torah values is difficult in this sort of cultural environment. It is not easy to impart the ideals of modesty and commitment in a society that idealizes immodesty and the thrill of the moment. The rabbi is competing with massive, ubiquitous industries that reflect and shape contemporary mores: fashion, entertainment, advertising, the media, the arts. Moral relativism is pervasive. Peer pressure, especially among the young and immature, is very strong.

And the fact is, the American family has been undergoing major changes. Everyone is aware of the decline of the traditional family composed of children, a father who goes to work, and a mother who stays home to care for home and children.

In 1993, the New York City Board of Education issued a draft of a resource guide for first-grade teachers. Known as the "Children of the Rainbow Curriculum," it was an effort to inculcate multicultural notions into New York City youngsters. I met with and corresponded with Dr. Leslie Agard-Jones, director of multicultural education, raising a number of issues that troubled me about the curriculum. One of the issues related to the nature of families.

The curriculum called on teachers to "support differing family structures." Since over eighty percent of the children in the New York public school system were considered to come from "non-traditional" families, teachers were told that they should be accepting of all family settings; that is, children raised by one parent, grandparents or relatives, foster parents, homosexual parents, etc. It was judged inappropriate to depict families consisting of two parents and children, since this might make children not raised in such families feel uncomfortable. I wrote to Dr. Agard-Jones on March 18, 1993, and made the following observations:

> Certainly, it is true that there are many kinds of families in our society. Whether this is good or bad, children should not be made to suffer through discriminatory

actions or words. On the other hand, a system which avoids making a value judgment is itself making a value judgment: namely, everything is good, everything is correct. I think, though, that this is not a good lesson to teach our children. We need to find a balance between maintaining a value system while at the same time not discriminating against those who no not share this system. . . . Does a child from a "traditional" family—who has a mother at home to care for him/her and a father who goes to work—does such a child feel left out by the curriculum? Even though such children are a small minority in the New York public school system, shouldn't they also be entitled to have a good feeling about their family arrangement?

It seems to me that the traditional family framework—modified to allow greater career opportunities for mothers and more home responsibilities for fathers—provides a structure for family cohesiveness and sociological stability. Although not all families will achieve this pattern, the ideal should nevertheless be respected and promoted. Yet, it is not fashionable to maintain this approach in various circles of American society. A rabbi, along with other religious Jews, will often feel that he is shouting into the wilderness. He is branded as being out of touch with modern times, even though he is espousing a progressive and advanced moral vision.

In an address entitled "The Lonely Man of Faith," Rabbi Joseph Soloveitchik expressed the dilemma of a religious person in the modern Western world. He stated that it was lonely being a person of faith in "modern society which is technically-minded, self-centered, and self-loving, almost in a sickly narcissistic fashion, scoring honor upon honor, piling up victory upon victory, reaching for the distant galaxies, and seeing in the here-and-now sensible world the only manifestation of being." Being a proponent of a God-given moral system can indeed make one feel lonely in our society: we teach I-thou and I–Eternal Thou, while the dominant forces in society drum in the I-it worldview.

Torah Judaism has not been afraid to stand alone throughout the centuries. It has stressed an elevated concept of human interrelationships based on modesty, shared respect, commitment to others. These values have been the framework of Jewish sexual morality and family life for millennia.

But contemporary sociological conditions have also influenced a large number of Jews. The general American patterns of interpersonal relationships and sexuality are also evident among Jews, especially those who are removed from religious observance. The age of brides and grooms at the time of their first marriages has gone up. Whereas it was once usual for people to marry while they were in their early twenties, it has become more common for them to be in their late twenties, thirties, and even older. Increasing numbers of couples simply live together outside the framework of marriage. In large segments of American society, this is considered normal—not shameful at all. More and more individuals live longer periods of their lives as singles. The rate of divorce has risen. The number of single-parent families has grown. The number of children growing up in homes with both a Jewish father and a Jewish mother has declined. While the situation in the Orthodox Jewish community is far more traditional, the negative trends of society also have had an impact on the Orthodox world.

Over the past thirty years, I have officiated at many weddings. Few of them involved a bride and groom who were both in their twenties or younger. The overwhelming majority of first marriages that I have performed were for couples where at least one of them was in their thirties; many such couples had been living with each other prior to the wedding.

The *New York Times* recently reported that the marriage rate in the United States has been declining. Couples have increasingly been choosing to live together without making a commitment to marriage. Another report stated that approximately thirty-five percent of those who get married do so without the expectation that their marriage will last a lifetime. The high divorce rate shakes confidence in the stability and permanence of marriage. A number of single people have told me that they have hesitated to make a marriage commitment because they were afraid the marriage might not last. It was safer to avoid marriage, they said, rather than to take the chance and then suffer failure.

Parents need to work hard to raise their children to avoid the pitfalls of contemporary sociological patterns. Not only must they provide a moral framework in the home, but they must choose educational and recreational settings where their children will be with peers who are also from families who care about religious values. A rabbi's duties include reminding parents of their responsibility for their children's spiritual well-being, reminding the community of the sanctity of marriage, counseling couples and families when they seek guidance, being available to partners of a marriage that is breaking up and moving toward divorce, striving to keep an inclusive atmosphere in the synagogue community so that all—

whether married, single, divorced, or widowed—may feel comfortable in the congregation.

During the late 1970s and early 1980s, I was quite active in the Commission on Synagogue Relations of the Federation of Jewish Philanthropies of New York. For several years, I was co-chairman of a committee ominously named the Committee on Marriage and Divorce. We eventually came to refer to it as the Committee on Jewish Family Life. We spent considerable time and effort addressing the situation of singles in the New York Jewish community. The committee encouraged synagogues to sponsor events for Jewish singles and to reach out to include them in synagogue life. Our own congregation sponsored weekly programs for Jewish singles in their middle years (forties and fifties) as well as groups for single parents. We have also sponsored Friday night dinners and Shabbat programs geared for singles. Many other congregations throughout Greater New York also instituted and expanded programs for Jewish singles.

The goal of these programs, stated or unstated, was to give Jewish singles opportunities to meet one another in the hope that marriages would result. Happily, some marriages did result from our various programs, although not as many as we would have liked. A considerable number of single people are not willing or able to make a full commitment to another person. They think: maybe someone better will come along. And when someone better does come along, they think: maybe this isn't the right one. Maybe the previous one was actually better for me. They vacillate through their twenties and thirties, sometimes throughout their lives. Meanwhile, the singles population grows, and needs the services of the community and the involvement of the rabbis.

Our committee at the Federation of Jewish Philanthropies also devoted considerable time to the area of premarital counseling. Since rabbis are regularly involved in interviewing couples for weddings, they need to have the necessary skills to sense problem areas that couples may be facing. Good rabbinic guidance can help alleviate future difficulties for the couple.

I remember interviewing a couple who planned to be married in our synagogue. During the course of the interview, I asked if there were any areas of conflict between them. They assured me that they never argued about anything, that they were totally in harmony with each other. I then asked the groom: "If you could change one thing about your bride, what would you change?" He immediately rattled off a list of negative traits that bothered him about her. She became livid. She retorted by listing a number of his negative traits that caused her annoyance. They proceeded to have a heated argument, as though oblivious of my presence. I gently interceded; I reminded them that they had told me that they were in perfect harmony with each other, that they never quarreled. They settled down and appeared to be somewhat embarrassed. I told them that they obviously had a lot of work to do before they would be ready to get married. They needed to be honest with each other, to state their true feelings about each other; without such candor, it would be unlikely for a marriage to survive. People have to be able to disagree, to criticize each other—but in a loving way.

I always tell couples that a good marriage requires love, honesty, patience, and a good sense of humor. Building a life together is a wonderful adventure, incredibly meaningful and satisfying. But to gain the most from marriage, each partner must be able to give fully to the relationship. When either or both of the marriage partners reneges on true commitment, the marriage is in trouble.

Over the years, I have interviewed a number of couples whose relationships were problematic. In some cases, one of the partners was far more religiously inclined than the other. In other cases, there were serious personality clashes: one was always on time, the other was perpetually late; one was neat, the other was sloppy; one was intense and aggressive, the other, easygoing and passive. In a few cases, one of the partners did almost all the talking, barely giving the other a chance to get in a few words. In one case, the man expressed the desire to have four or five children, while the woman said that she did not intend to have any children! These couples all came to see me after they had already decided to get married. They obviously thought that they could easily overcome the troublesome aspects of their relationship once they were married. In such cases, I have explained to couples that marriages should not be entered on the assumption that one will be able to change a spouse's beliefs or behaviors. Sometimes, changes do in fact occur; but one may not count on this. Rather, the couple needs to work on the problems in advance of marriage. They need to assure themselves that they are prepared to live a lifetime with their spouses just as they are. When couples spend the time and effort needed to resolve problems, they are able to enter their marriages with much more confidence and happiness. When they gloss over their problems, they often have to struggle with them throughout their married lives together.

It happens that some marriages do not succeed. Sometimes a couple reaches the point where a decision for divorce is reached. When both partners agree to the divorce and arrange for an amicable separation, the trauma to themselves and their children—though great—is ameliorated. When the divorce involves ugly battles for custody of children and distribution of assets, then the level of trauma can be quite severe for all concerned.

In my experience as a rabbi, a number of couples have come to me for marriage counseling. They often have come, though, when they were already on the verge of divorce. In those cases where I thought marriage counseling could help the couple, I have referred them to marriage counselors. In those cases where civil divorce was imminent, I offered whatever guidance and friendship I could, and advised them also to arrange for a Jewish religious divorce.

In rare cases, I have had to deal with situations where one of the spouses refused to participate in a religious divorce ceremony. The refusal was motivated by bitterness, vindictiveness, or a conscious disregard of religious law. In almost all of these cases, the situation was ultimately resolved in accordance with Jewish law.

It goes without saying that a rabbi shares in the suffering of congregants who struggle through a breakup of their marriages. This is especially so if the rabbi has known the couple for years and may even have officiated at their wedding. Many long and painful hours have been spent by rabbis in divorce counseling.

Whether it be pre-marital, marital or divorce counseling, a rabbi can be a valuable resource to members of his congregation and community. Since most rabbis are not professional psychologists or social workers, they generally should not attempt long-term counseling. But they can (and should) be good diagnosticians. They can provide useful insights to help clarify and resolve real or potential conflicts and when the cases before them are beyond their scope, they should be able to refer couples to competent professional counselors.

The strength, purity and happiness of Jewish family life are of utmost significance to the vitality of the Jewish people. As workers on behalf of Kenesset Yisrael, rabbis must invest much time, patience and talent on behalf of the well-being of Jewish families.

5

Ḥesed—Compassion

The daily morning prayer service includes the recitation of Psalm 146. The psalm praises God: He performs justice for the oppressed, provides bread for the hungry, frees those who are bound, gives vision to the blind, straightens the bent. In all of these cases, the person has a deficiency and the Lord comes to repair it. But here the psalm inserts the clause "God loves the righteous"; and then continues by praising God for protecting strangers and assisting the orphan and the widow. Why is the phrase "God loves the righteous" included in the midst of these descriptions of God's mercies?

Taking this phrase in the same pattern as the other phrases, we may understand it to mean that a righteous person has a deficiency that God repairs by supplying love. On one level, this may mean that a righteous person, because of his commitment to righteousness, must often stand alone. He may feel alienated from and ostracized by others, who do not share his moral vision. Thus, the psalm teaches that God comes to fill in the deficiency: He loves the righteous, He provides the love that the righteous person does not always receive from other members of society.

I think that the phrase can also be understood in another way. It may refer to a lack in the righteous person's ability to love others. Viewing life as a set of ritual obligations that must be fulfilled, he may be more committed to these rituals than to people. Indeed, people may very well get in the way of his religious observance, so he becomes annoyed with them. Ultimately, a righteous person may even come to disdain those who are not equally committed to fulfilling the religious precepts. His self-righteousness is characterized by scorn of others, not love; thus, he lacks the quality of love. The psalm teaches, therefore, that God must intervene by infusing the righteous with love.

Rabbi Hayyim Yosef David Azulai, one of the leading sages of the eighteenth century, explained the difference between the words *tsaddik* (righteous) and *ḥasid* (pious). The righteous person clings to the letter of the law; the pious person does more than the law requires. Whereas a *tsaddik* will do what the law demands, a *ḥasid* will fulfill the law in a spirit of love and selflessness. If the chief characteristic of a *tsaddik* is justice, the main characteristic of a *ḥasid* is love.

Applying this analysis to Psalm 146, God recognizes that the righteous person, in spite of his many virtues, lacks the quality of true piety, that is to say, love. So God "loves the righteous," providing the quality of love in such individuals so that they will be morally repaired, and can become pious.

Early in my career as a rabbi, I wrote myself an observation about the nature of the religious personality. I have kept this note in my desk all these years, and refer to it from time to time. It is a basic lesson that needs to be remembered constantly.

> When an artist becomes self-conscious that he is an artist, he loses his quality of being a genuine artist. The same is true of a religious personality. An artist, a poet, a religious person is always groping, trying to express some deep feelings or ideas for which his expressions are inadequate. He tries again and again and always—at least to himself—fails. Once he thinks he has succeeded, if only for an instant, in that instant he is no longer an artist, a poet, a religious personality. His vanity has obscured his humility. But it is humility and the sense of inadequacy which serve as the foundation of spiritual greatness.

Alan Watts, in his book *The Supreme Identity*, writes:

> The most spiritual people are the most human. They are natural and easy in manner; they give themselves no airs; they interest themselves in ordinary everyday matters, and are not forever talking and thinking about religion. For them there is no difference between spirituality and usual life, and to their awakened insight the lives of the most humdrum and earth-bound people are as much in harmony with the infinite as their own.

These are sentiments that every serious student of religiosity will appreciate.

Nonetheless, in religious life as in society in general, everyone does not achieve these lofty standards. While self-righteousness, hypocrisy, and moral weakness are repugnant in anyone, they are especially offensive in people who claim to be religious.

In my address as outgoing president of the Rabbinical Council of America (June 16, 1992), I spoke to the rabbis at the convention on the topic of authentic religiosity: The following is an excerpt from that speech:

> Religion has two faces. One face is that of saintliness, idealism, holiness, and selflessness. But the other face is one of hatred, cruelty, selfishness, and egotism. Within the world of religion, one can find the most exemplary human beings; and one also can find inquisitors. In his play *The Father*, August Strindberg has one of his characters state: "It is strange that as soon as you begin to talk about God and love, your voice becomes hard and your eyes full of hate." This is a reflection of the second face of religion, when a person cloaks himself in religious garb but actually is filled with hatred and cruelty.
>
> I think all of us can think of examples of religion at its worst as well as examples of religion at its best. Each of us has seen the two faces of religion.
>
> But I think we all would agree that every person who claims to be religious actually thinks himself to reflect the loving and beautiful face of religion. Even those who are cruel and hateful believe themselves to be righteous and good. Perhaps it is a feature of human nature for individuals to delude themselves, to judge themselves in the best possible light.
>
> But what are the standards by which we can measure true piety? How can we know if we are living religion at its best?
>
> The Talmud (Berakhot 4a) offers us a framework by which we can evaluate genuine piety. In Psalm 86, King David asks God to guard his soul *ki ḥasid ani*, "for I am a saint." The word ḥasid denotes true and selfless piety. It is religion at its best. Several opinions are offered by the Talmud in order to understand exactly why King David referred to himself as a ḥasid.

The first observation is: "Said David before God: Master of the universe, am I not a hasid? All the other kings of the east and west sleep until three hours [of sunlight], but I arise at midnight to thank you."

What was King David saying? All other kings slept late, they were concerned with their own honor and comfort. But King David awoke in the middle of the night in order to praise God. In other words, he did not stand on ceremony, thinking that as a king he was entitled to pamper himself. He demonstrated that his commitment to God was his primary concern.

It is not always easy for a person to be able to distinguish true piety from false piety. One must be scrupulously self-critical in order to root out egocentrism. One needs to be exceedingly careful in evaluating his own motives. Is he acting as a hasid or is he only promoting himself while hiding in the clothing of a hasid?

It sometimes happens that people engage in in-fighting, power struggles, defamation of character—all in the name of religion. They spread controversy and dissension, yet they pose as peace-makers and lovers of God and Israel. Such behavior, though, is not a reflection of the true ideals of religion: it is demagoguery, it is false. It needs to be exposed for what it is.

The Talmud offers another explanation of why King David was a hasid. "Said David before God: Master of the universe, am I not a hasid? All the other kings of the east and west sit in large groups for their honor, whereas my hands are dirtied with menstrual blood in order to permit a wife to her husband."

King David dealt with difficult halakhic issues and did not seek to shirk his own duty. One must have the ability to take responsibility, to argue his case. One must not fold under pressure or lose heart due to opposition.

King David's hasidut was manifested not only in his courage to take personal responsibility, but also in his concern for basic human situations. He did not say that he was too important or too good to deal with the nitty-gritty of human life. He got his hands dirty. He made his judgments based on first-hand experience, not on theoretical knowledge. Rabbis also must get their hands dirty. They must deal with complicated and troubling cases. They do not have the luxury of hiding away in safe havens.

The Talmud offers a third criterion for being a ḥasid. "Whatever I do, I first consult Mephiboshet, my teacher, and ask him: Mephiboshet, my teacher, have I judged correctly? Have I punished fairly? Have I vindicated fairly? Was I correct in my judgments of purity and impurity? And I was not embarrassed [to consult him]." King David was willing to face criticism and correction. He was interested in finding truth, not in maintaining his own position at any cost.

There are those who take a position and then are ashamed to back down—even when they are wrong. They will fabricate every kind of argument to bolster their position, no matter how absurd. While pretending to argue for the glory of God, they actually argue only for their own glory."

In the kabbalistic system of sefirot, the level above Yesod (foundation) is Ḥesed (compassion). Ḥesed is the essential ingredient in being a *ḥasid*, a genuinely pious person. It is a manifestation of love, kindness, deep concern for others. Ḥesed is the underlying spirit of halakhah, Jewish law.

In talmudic times, two great rabbinic schools found themselves in conflict. The school of Shammai tended to be stricter in its rulings. The school of Hillel was generally more lenient. The Talmud (Eruvin 13b) reports that a heavenly voice announced that both schools represented the word of the living God—but that the law should follow the school of Hillel. Why? Because the school of Hillel was humbler, more respectful. Jewish law, in the final analysis, must reflect an attitude of Ḥesed and sympathy. Its purpose is to help people live happier, more meaningful lives.

In the introduction to one of his volumes of responsa (*Mishpetei Uziel*, 5700), Rabbi Benzion Uziel noted that Jewish law incorporates both righteousness and justice, compassion and truth. How can these concepts function simultaneously?

> The fundamental teaching of the laws of justice is that one may not show compassion in justice, but should uphold the law whatever the consequences. On the other hand, we are taught to do that which is good and upright, and we may compel behavior that is beyond the letter of the law. The question stands in all its strength: how can we blend these two opposites? The short but profoundly poignant answer is: The Lord is with the judge; the holy presence of the God of justice hovers above the head of the judge as he sits in judgment, filled with fear and trembling.

In his own halakhic rulings, Rabbi Uziel admirably demonstrated how one may be loyal to legal texts and traditions while at the same time being infused with the spirit of love and compassion.

A guiding principle of halakhah is the verse: "Her ways are the ways of pleasantness, and all her pathways are peace" (Proverbs 3:17). The Talmud teaches that Torah scholars are to increase peace in the world. By teaching and applying the laws of the Torah, they make the qualities of love and compassion more prevalent in society.

The halakhah is a manifestation of the will of God, the ultimate Source of lovingkindness.

A rabbi is the halakhic authority for his community. He receives questions on a broad range of issues—ritual, ethical, philosophical. In many cases, he feels competent to provide answers immediately or after some research. When he is not confident that his answer is correct, he consults other rabbis, especially those who have gained the reputation for halakhic expertise in the area of the question at hand. But ultimately, the rabbi is obligated to arrive at an authoritative answer and respond to the person who asked the question. A rabbi who makes halakhic rulings without having the necessary erudition and sound judgment is presumptuous. A rabbi who shirks the responsibility of making halakhic rulings is a coward.

In my own experience as a rabbi of a large congregation, I have received many questions on matters of Jewish law. A significant number have pertained to ritual issues, such as kashruth, the Sabbath, Passover, the laws of family purity. Others have dealt with broader issues: conversion to Judaism, relations with family members who have married out of the faith, laws of marriage and divorce. A number have related to issues of congregational policy, such as the role of women in synagogue ritual. Some have concerned life-and-death issues: abortion, treatment of the terminally ill, organ transplantation.

A rabbi learns early in his career that there is a gap between the theoretical knowledge he obtained in rabbinical school and the practical knowledge needed to answer real halakhic questions. In the world of yeshivot, the emphasis is placed on studying the Talmud and its commentaries. Even when time is devoted to halakhic texts, the method of study is often theoretical. And even when classes are devoted specifically to practical issues, the student lacks the experience to know how to communicate the halakhot to specific human beings, to specific congregations and communities. It is never enough simply to know halakhic texts: one must also be sensitive to the particular circumstances of each question.

A midrash tells that Moses studied the Torah on Mount Sinai for forty days and nights, under the tutelage of God Himself. And yet, the moment Moses learned something, he seemed immediately to forget it. "Lord of the universe," cried Moses in despair, "forty days have I devoted to studying the Torah without having profited by it." God then instructed Moses to descend to the Israelites and teach them the Torah.

What is the meaning of this midrash? I believe it alludes to the fact that the Torah can be learned only in the context of human situations, through practical experience. Studying the Torah on a mountaintop, even with God as teacher, is not sufficient. The Torah's message lives and means something only in the particular circumstances of peoples' lives. Certainly, Moses did learn much from God; but he felt as though he knew nothing. So God instructed him to go to the Israelites, where Moses would have to apply his theoretical knowledge to real situations.

Rabbis learn to understand and apply halakhah by dealing with questions raised by members of their communities. To issue proper halakhic decisions, one must not only be versed in the relevant halakhic literature, but must also be imbued with Ḥesed. A rabbinical decisor must be able to look into the eyes of those who ask him questions; he must understand their concerns, feel their struggles, sense the implications of what his answer will mean to their lives. A rabbi must be able to reach a decision and take the responsibility for it.

Taking responsibility is always important. But it is vital especially in matters of public policy. When I was president of the Rabbinical Council of America (1990–1992), we issued a health-care proxy developed by Rabbi Dr. Moses Tendler, chairman of our medical ethics committee. The proxy accepts brain death (the total cessation of activity of the brain stem) as the definition of death. Thus, it enables the possibility of organ transplants, providing the opportunity for saving many lives.

The health-care proxy immediately came under fire from a number of rabbis, both within and outside of the Rabbinical Council of America. Some complained: why did we have to take a stand on the controversial issue of brain-stem death and organ transplants? I responded in an article in the *RCA Record* (September/October 1991):

> The issue has to be decided. Who will do it? Who will take the responsibility in these matters of life and death? The fact is that members of the RCA serve hundreds of communities and are faced with life and death questions regularly. Should we not assume responsibility to answer such questions? Is it morally defensible to stay neutral, when neutrality will almost always lead to a do-nothing position?

We provided the halakhic and medical reasoning to defend our position. Some critics, though, argued that as long as the heart is beating, even by artificial means, a person is still alive. I asked one of these critics: "If a human being were decapitated, and we were able to attach his headless body to machines so that his heart continued to beat and his lungs continued to inhale and exhale, is that headless person still alive according to halakhah?" The rabbi answered without hesitation: "He is still alive!" In relating this conversation to the RCA membership, I wrote:

> I confess that to me this position is absurd. To rule that this headless corpse is alive because machines can pump air into its organs is a position I would not want the RCA to have to defend. To reject the brain-stem death definition (which is tantamount to decapitation, in the sense that the brain is no longer alive and does not control bodily functions) is to condemn to death people who need vital organ transplants in order to live.

Some critics stated that the brain-stem definition of death was incorrect. They ruled, therefore, that no doctor should perform a transplant of a vital organ from a brain-stem dead person, and no one should agree to donate organs in such circumstances. But, they said, it was permissible to receive organ transplants! In response to this, I wrote:

> It is morally repugnant to claim that taking organs from a brain dead person is murder (or possibly murder), and then rule that it is permissible to accept such organ donations. Those who reject the brain-stem death definition should follow the consequences of that position—no vital organ transplants should be received by them or their loved ones or others over whom they have halakhic authority.

I once asked a rabbinic critic who had signed his name to a document opposing the RCA position: "If a member of your family or congregation was dying and in need of a heart transplant, and if the heart of a brain-stem dead person became available, would you allow your loved one to die rather than receive the heart transplant?" He answered: "I would ask the family involved not to ask me for a halakhic ruling. I would ask them to call Rabbi Tendler." I reminded him that he had signed his name on a document negating Rabbi Tendler's position. He replied: "I felt compelled to do so to assuage some of my colleagues." It did not occur to him that he had a responsibility to everyone who would see his signature among those who opposed transplantation of vital organs. It seems to me a lack of halakhic integrity to sign one's name in opposition to a policy that one would advise people to follow if the occasion arose.

Halakhic decisions, if they are to be taken seriously by the public, must be taken seriously by the rabbis who issue them. Just as presumptuousness is reprehensible in one who makes a halakhic ruling, so is spinelessness.

During my tenure as president of the Rabbinical Council of America, we dealt with a number of thorny halakhic questions. We not only issued our health-care proxy, but we had conferences and discussions relating to homosexuals and homosexuality, conversion to Judaism, outreach to intermarried couples, and prenuptial agreements. Our goal was to study topics thoroughly so that we could issue proper halakhic and moral guidance to our communities. To shy away from difficult and controversial issues would be an abdication of rabbinic responsibility.

In January 1992, the Rabbinical Council of America sponsored a series of conferences throughout the United States on the theme of Orthodox responsibility to intermarried Jews. The general purpose of these conferences was to develop a national policy for the RCA, in the hope that the Orthodox rabbinate would take a leadership role in this area. Our position needed to go beyond condemning intermarriage and lamenting the spread of religious assimilation. It was hoped that we could develop constructive ideas for reaching out to intermarried couples and families, so that at least some of them might be brought back within the halakhic fold.

These conferences were well attended and well publicized. They were an attempt to mobilize the Orthodox rabbinate to grapple with a very serious problem. But elements within the Orthodox rabbinate, including some members of the RCA, felt that we should never have acknowledged the problem of intermarriage. We were attacked in right-wing circles as having made peace with intermarriage and allegedly being ready to compromise halakhic standards. In my RCA diary for February 3, 1992, I wrote:

> Needless to say, this is all quite absurd and foolish. We are obviously just as opposed to intermarriage as anybody else on the "right." The difference is that we recognize the reality that the intermarriage rate has passed 50% and requires a forceful Orthodox response. Simply to condemn others or to pretend that the problem is only a problem of the non-Orthodox—these are ludicrous and untenable positions. They reflect moral weakness and self-righteousness. It seems to me that it is about time that the Orthodox community became more vocal in asserting its own leadership, and its own willingness to provide religious leadership for the entire community. It is a sad commentary on Orthodox life when a conference of such great significance to our community is criticized by self-serving, self-righteous publicity seekers.

A number of Talmud teachers at Yeshiva University informed me of their dismay that the RCA had become involved in the question of outreach to intermarried couples. We had a meeting, at which I explained that we were as opposed to intermarriage as they were. Many thousands of Jews were marrying out of the faith, I said, including members of the Orthodox community. A large percentage of these people would be lost to the Jewish people. But some of them might be brought back if we showed a greater degree of understanding, openness, compassion. We should not leave the impression that only non-Orthodox rabbis are interested and available to guide such individuals. As responsible spokesmen for Torah and halakhah, we should encourage intermarried couples to come to us. Perhaps we would be able to bring them around; perhaps we would be able to arrange halakhic conversions when appropriate; perhaps we would reconnect some of them and their children with Kenesset Yisrael.

The Talmud teachers were not swayed by my arguments. One of them suggested that only a select few talmudic sages were authorized to make decisions on such topics, and that the RCA should have consulted them in order to establish policy. I responded: "Please tell me the name of an `authorized talmudic sage' who has regularly dealt with intermarried couples, who has shared their emotional and family struggles, who has an understanding of their sense of Jewishness; who has spent long hours consoling and counseling their parents. I do not know of such an individual. The only ones I know who have any clue as to the reality of intermarriage are synagogue rabbis who actually confront individuals from their communities who are intermarrying or intermarried."

The Talmud teachers were still not convinced. They continued to protest the RCA's involvement in the question of intermarriage. The matter soon became so controversial that many members of the RCA, even some who had originally supported our initiative, wanted the RCA to drop the subject. Interest waned, and the issue faded from the agenda.

The Talmud (Gittin 56a) records that the scrupulousness of Rabbi Zekhariah ben Abkulos led to the destruction of the Temple of Jerusalem. The rabbis of his time were presented with a serious halakhic problem. The Roman emperor had sent an animal to be sacrificed in the Temple. But a traitorous Jew had blemished the animal's eye, making it unfit for an offering. The rabbis felt they should offer the sacrifice anyway, knowing that if they did not, the emperor would become enraged and would attack the Jews. But Zekhariah ben Abkulos objected: "People will say that it is permitted to offer blemished sacrifices." The rabbis replied: "Let us murder the traitorous Jew, so that he will be unable to report back to the emperor." But Zekhariah objected again: "Putting a blemish in the eye of an animal is not punishable by death." So the rabbis, deferring to Zekhariah's objections, rejected the emperor's offering. As expected, the emperor felt insulted and took the Jewish refusal of his offering as a sign of revolt. He sent his troops to sack Jerusalem and raze the Temple.

The instinct of the rabbis was right. They should have offered the sacrifice or found some other way to avoid antagonizing the emperor. But they were cowed by the objections of Zekhariah ben Abkulos. In narrow technical terms, Zekhariah was right. But there were greater issues at stake that also needed to be factored into the decision. Zekhariah lacked the courage to go beyond the letter of the law. Who are we, he must have thought, to overrule decisions of our sages of previous generations? What right do we have to sidestep the law, or to give a broader interpretation of the law? Zekhariah's obsequiousness led to the destruction of Jerusalem. And yet, his fellow rabbis were also culpable. Why didn't they have the courage to overrule Zekhariah? Why did they give in to his objections? The fact is that all the rabbis lacked the confidence to make big, unprecedented decisions. Zekhariah was afraid to deviate from precedent. His colleagues were afraid to appear more lenient or liberal than Zekhariah. So the Jewish people suffered a horrible catastrophe; their homeland was destroyed, and they were sent into an exile that lasted nearly nineteen hundred years until Jewish sovereignty was once again established in the land of Israel.

In order for the halakhah to function as a source of life and compassion for the people, it is imperative that halakhic authorities demonstrate great knowledge, understanding, sensitivity—and courage. New challenges arise in every generation. It is the responsibility of the halakhic community of each generation to respond to these challenges without fear.

True, halakhic leadership must confront new and changing realities with wisdom and creativity. But this does not mean that change for the sake of change is halakhically acceptable. Rather, one needs to weigh the claims of tradition and the claims of modernity; one needs to evaluate the implications of halakhic decisions and innovations. The halakhic process is dynamic; it must balance many considerations. And even if a certain halakhic position can be defended, this does not mean it should therefore be implemented automatically. Halakhah functions within a communal framework, and must play its role in maintaining harmony and a spirit of Ḥesed.

An area of halakhic inquiry that has proven to be controversial relates to the role of women in synagogue life. Different attitudes are apparent among the Orthodox. I recently had a conversation with a rabbinic colleague on the issue of women serving in positions of leadership in the Orthodox community. Specifically, we were discussing the halakhic basis of women serving as presidents and officers of synagogues, day schools, and other communal institutions. My colleague dismissed these possibilities. He argued that women had not held these offices in past generations, and to change this pattern would therefore violate Jewish tradition. I reminded him that a hundred years ago, most women—Jewish and non-Jewish—were not allowed to vote in most of the countries of the world, let alone be elected to public office. Yet, a social revolution has occurred during the past few generations. Today we are confronting a very different question than that which was confronted by halakhic sages a hundred and more years ago. While we must be rooted in halakhic sources and traditions, we must also be sensitive enough to know how to apply eternal halakhic principles to a new set of circumstances. We ought not to conduct halakhic discussion under the pretense that nothing has changed. While some halakhists may still rule in favor of restricting women's participation, others may find halakhic justification to expand women's involvement in communal leadership.

Within our own congregation, for example, women are elected to the Board of Trustees and do serve in leadership roles. We have also instituted a number of frameworks for women's personal participation in synagogue rituals: a Bat Mitzvah ceremony, a women's Megillah reading on Purim, a women's Hakafoth ceremony on Simḥat Torah, periodic women's prayer services, conducted by and for women only. In all cases, we have not only insisted on maintaining proper halakhic standards, but we have also been sensitive to the feelings of members of the congregation. We did not implement new practices until we first created an intellectual and social climate that would be receptive to them. We had classes, public discussions, meetings, sermons. When the women's services were finally started, we already had developed a strong positive consensus within the congregation. We experienced little or no controversy.

On the other hand, there are Orthodox congregations where these practices are felt to be unneeded and where the public sentiment is against expanding ritual opportunities for women. In those communities, I agree, such innovations should not be made—at least not until the community at large supports them. Halakhah is not simply a matter of legal argumentation; it must also take into consideration communal practice, tradition, sentiment. The rabbi of each congregation needs to take responsibility for the implementation of halakhah in his community.

He must foster an openness of spirit, an ability to see Torah with a fresh and inquiring mind.

6

Gevurah—Strength, Heroism

One of the late members of our congregation, Dr. Silvano Arieti, was a distinguished psychiatrist and author. In his book *The Will to Be Human*, he described an incident that occurred in 1922, when he was a fourth-grader growing up in Italy. At that time, Mussolini was in power and fascism was rapidly becoming the popular ideology of the country. Arieti's own teacher was an avid member of the Fascist Party. The pervasive propaganda influenced the young Jewish child to write a poem lauding the virtues of fascism. (This was before the emergence of the blatantly anti-Jewish features of Italian fascism.)

The young Arieti read the poem to his class and was highly praised by his teacher and classmates. Filled with pride, he read the poem that evening to his father. But his father, who strongly opposed the fascist ideology, scolded his son for having written such a poem. The little boy was stunned. He had received such positive reactions from his teacher and friends, and yet his own father criticized him.

As time passed, Arieti came to appreciate his father's wisdom. His own disillusionment with fascism intensified as he contemplated the fascist chants proclaiming that Mussolini was always right, that he could make no mistakes. The young Arieti realized that this ideology could not be true and that it was, in fact, quite dangerous.

In the late 1930s, Dr. Arieti fled fascist Italy and settled in New York, where he became a prominent psychiatrist. His childhood experiences helped him to understand how human beings internalize external influences.

When we are children, our parents give us commands. Although we lack the experience and wisdom to determine whether these commands are good or bad, we internalize them because they emanate from parents, whom we trust. As we grow older, the instructions we received from parents and other authority figures become part of our own inner system of self-control. This is a healthy and necessary process, which Dr. Arieti calls "endocracy." Endocracy means that we have learned the basic rules of our civilization and have willingly incorporated them into our own system of life.

But Dr. Arieti also writes of endocratic surplus. This occurs when we internalize too much from external sources, thus losing our autonomy. We judge and act according to prevailing values or influences imposed on us by others. Throughout history, people have been victims of endocratic surplus when they have uncritically absorbed external ideologies, and have not freely evaluated what they were absorbing. This is how the child Arieti had become enamored of fascism under the influence of his teacher.

A century and a half ago, many Americans were proponents of slavery—not because they were innately bad people, but because they were raised to think that slavery was not morally repugnant. Indeed, throughout history, people have believed absurd and dangerous things because they did not have the inner strength and clarity to reject prevailing attitudes. Endocratic surplus is not something that existed only in past eras, but is a factor in all of our lives. Individuals absorb prejudices and false assumptions from their family, peers, and general culture.

The more endocratic surplus we have, the less free we are. We lose our ability to think critically; we live according to the thoughts and emotions projected into us by others. To be spiritually healthy human beings, we need to maintain a proper balance: we must recognize those concepts and rules that have been internalized to our benefit and with our ultimate approval; and we must also be able to identify endocratic surplus, which deprives us of our freedom and autonomy.

We all necessarily learn from others. Civilization depends on the orderly communication and transmission of modes of thinking and behaving. We depend on the authority of others for many things. Yet, genuine authority must be authoritative—not authoritarian. A person gains authority with us by winning our respect and trust. But an authoritarian approach threatens mature, free human life. While authoritativeness fosters a healthy endocracy, authoritarianism often engenders an unhealthy endocratic surplus.

It seems to me that Judaism teaches us to maintain a proper balance. On the one hand, we need endocracy; we need the laws and traditions that infuse our lives with righteousness and holiness. Healthy endocracy means that we constantly deepen our knowledge and experience, so that we willingly and lovingly accept the authority of Torah and mitzvot. On the other hand, we constantly need to be vigilant not to be overtaken by endocratic surplus, not to submit uncritically to authoritarianism. We need an openness of spirit, an ability to see Torah with fresh and inquiring minds. Religion is not an escape from decision-making, but a constant challenge, calling on us to study, think, and make choices.

In the kabbalistic scheme of sefirot, Gevurah (strength, heroism) is parallel to Ḥesed, compassion. Gevurah entails the ability to think for oneself and have the courage of one's convictions. It opposes authoritarianism, calling on us to take responsibility for our decisions, to develop and maintain a strong moral sense, to distinguish between endocracy and endocratic surplus.

This aspect of Gevurah is sometimes seen as being in conflict with traditional religious teachings. Orthodoxy seems to demand faithful allegiance to a large body of laws and traditions, sharply limiting the individual's freedom of thought and action. Moreover, it is argued in some circles that Orthodoxy depends on a hierarchical and authoritarian framework: individuals must submit uncritically to the rulings and interpretations of the most learned rabbis.

It is true that Torah law and tradition do present boundaries to our behavior; but I believe that these boundaries are in the category of healthy endocracy. We study and attempt to comprehend the profundity of our religious laws and traditions, thereby internalizing them as valuable and powerful sources of moral life. Only if we observe religious precepts blindly, without attempting to understand and integrate their meanings, do we find ourselves in the category of endocratic surplus. Only if we entirely surrender our autonomy to rabbinic authority do we forfeit our spiritual independence. True Orthodoxy does not make these demands on us. Rather, it fosters a spirit of allegiance to tradition and at the same time a demand for critical intellectual analysis.

I recently dealt with the general theme of Orthodoxy and diversity of opinion in an essay for the *Newsletter of the Rabbinic Alumni of Yeshiva University* (May 1998). The following are excerpts from that article:

> The Talmud (Berakhot 58a) teaches that one is required to make a special blessing when witnessing a huge throng of Jews, praising God who is *Hakham ha-razim*, the One who understands the root and inner thoughts of each individual. Their thoughts are not alike and their appearance is not alike. God created each person to be unique. He expected and wanted diversity of thought, and we bless God for this diversity.
>
> Sodom represents the antithesis of this ideal. The Talmud relates that the Sodomites placed visitors in a bed. If the person was too short, he was stretched until he fit the bed. If he was too tall, his legs were cut off so that he could fit the bed. This parable is not merely referring to physical uniformity. The people of Sodom wanted everyone to be the same, to think alike. They fostered and enforced conformity.
>
> Respect for individuality and diversity is a necessity of healthy human life. We each have unique talents and insights, and we require the spiritual climate that allows us to grow, to be creative, to contribute to humanity's treasury of ideas and knowledge.
>
> The Torah grants individuals great freedom, but it also provides boundaries beyond which the individual may not trespass. When freedom becomes license, it damages

our community. On the other hand, when authoritarianism attempts to quash individual freedom, the dignity and sanctity of the individual are violated.

Some years ago, I visited a great Torah luminary in Israel who told me that people stopped attending his classes after he had made a controversial halakhic suggestion. A concerted effort was made by a group of right-wing extremists to discredit the rabbi, to undermine his support in his community. We don't have to go to Israel for such cases. We each can think of similar examples.

There is a subtle—and not so subtle—process of coercion. Decisions are being made as to which Orthodox individuals are "acceptable" and which are not. This process is insidious and is unhealthy for Orthodoxy. It deprives all of us of meaningful discussion and debate. It intimidates people from taking independent and original positions, for fear of being ostracized or isolated. The fear to dissent from the "acceptable" positions is palpable. But if we are not allowed to think independently, if we may not ask questions and raise alternatives, then we as a community suffer a loss of vitality and dynamism. Fear and timidity become our hallmark.

We need to foster a climate of open discussion and debate. We must resist and condemn efforts to impose conformity—we will not be fitted into the bed of Sodom. We must give communal support to diversity within the halakhic framework, so that people will not feel intimidated to say things publicly and sign their names to public documents.

We need to draw on the wisdom and inspiration of men and women spanning the generations, from communities throughout the world. We need to highlight the wide variety of Orthodox models so as to deepen our own religiosity and understanding; and so as to present Orthodoxy to ourselves and to the world as a living, dynamic, intellectually alive way of life.

A rabbi, especially a modern Orthodox rabbi, must constantly remind himself of the quality of Gevurah. One needs the courage to articulate well-reasoned opinions without fear of intimidation from those who may disagree. Within Orthodoxy, authoritarianism has been increasing; an unofficial but active "thought police" exists. On the other hand, attacks from the non-Orthodox have also become more strident. The only way to avoid being criticized is to remain silent; but then one would be criticized for remaining silent, for being afraid to take a stand!

Over the years, I have received my share of attacks and criticisms from people—right and left of me—who have disagreed with my positions. This is part of the nature of public discourse and responsibility. No matter how reasonable and sound one's own opinions may seem, it is inevitable that someone will disagree with them. It is sad, though, when critics, in their zeal to refute the arguments of others, resort to name-calling, misstatements, yellow journalism. I have had to deal with reporters who were more intent on finding scandal and controversy than on telling the truth; publishers who defended their reporters, even when it was demonstrated that the reporters were lying or badly mistaken; critics who preferred to attack me personally rather than address the ideas I had presented. I have often found consolation in the words of the late chief rabbi of the Island of Rhodes, Rabbi Reuben Eliyahu Israel: "Do not be upset when you are criticized unjustly, since many times you are also praised unjustly!"

In May 1991, at the conclusion of my first year as president of the Rabbinical Council of America, I wrote a letter to my colleagues in which I said:

> Since becoming President of the RCA, I have been attacked in the media for being a "hard-line Orthodox" spokesman, a right-winger; I have also been attacked for being a left-winger on the periphery of Orthodoxy. After reading the various articles, I sometimes look in the mirror to try to find out who I really am! I have learned, though, that what is important is not what the media say, but what we are, what we teach, and what we do. We need to be true to ourselves and faithful in our commitment to Torah and to the people of Israel. I have learned that it is important to formulate a consensus within our ranks, to promote that consensus, and to do our best to influence the Jewish people for the better. There are always those who will disagree for various reasons. They will attack us and misrepresent us. But we cannot let this nonsense deter us or sap our strength and energy. On the contrary, we need to work with a clear vision of where we are going and a steadfast determination to reach that goal.

Henry Adams offered an interesting way to distinguish a politician from a statesman. A politician, he wrote, is one who attempts to determine what people want, and then shapes his opinions accordingly. On the other hand, a statesman is one who formulates a well-reasoned policy and then attempts to shape public opinion so that it becomes receptive to it. A rabbi—indeed, any proper public figure—should strive to be a statesman rather than a politician. Those who pander to the pressures and moods of the public will find soon enough that the public is fickle. Today one policy is popular, and tomorrow another policy gains public approbation. A rabbi must have the knowledge, insight, and fortitude to lead intelligently; if he merely follows the path of least resistance, he betrays the responsibilities of his position.

I have worked with rabbis who have been politicians rather than statesmen. They have feared to take stands that would put them at odds with members of their congregation or would antagonize segments of the community. Their statements are "safe" and bland, unoriginal and unchallenging. To be sure, it is no virtue to be controversial just for the sake of the notoriety. But when one genuinely believes that a particular idea or policy is correct, then he should be prepared to explain it and defend it. He needs to assume the role of statesman.

Rabbi Joseph B. Soloveitchik, in a lecture on the role of the rabbi (May 18, 1955), commented: (Quoted from Aaron Rakeffet-Rothkoff, ed., *The Rav: The World of Rabbi Joseph B. Soloveitchik*, Hoboken, N.J.: Ktav Publishing House, 1999, vol. 2, pp. 47, 52.)

> It is not sufficient for the rabbi to know Torah and possess the competence to issue halakhic decisions. The religious leader must not only be a scholar and teacher, but he also must be a hero who has a firm hold on spiritual strength and courage. . . . The rabbi must be the symbol of fearlessness.

From time to time, criticisms are raised against rabbis by members of the community: Why don't rabbis assert more leadership? Why aren't they more learned, more confident of their Torah decisions? Why are they politicians rather than statesmen? But, generally speaking, these questions should not be addressed only to the rabbis, for to a certain extent rabbis reflect the spiritual climate of their congregation and community. A congregation that values freedom of expression gives its rabbi an impetus to be more creative and original. A congregation that wants to foster authoritarianism will attempt to mold its rabbi in this image. A rabbi's ability to function properly is correlated to the support or lack of support he receives from his congregation. Having said this, it is still primarily the rabbi's obligation to fulfill his rabbinic mission.

A rabbi should be kind, gentle, and compassionate; but not wishy-washy. He should be strong, confident, and persistent; but not authoritarian. I have had the good fortune to know a number of rabbis who lived up to these statesmenlike standards.

Rabbi Israel Salanter, one of the great rabbis of nineteenth-century Europe, quipped that any rabbi whose congregation did not want to fire him was no rabbi; and any rabbi who let his congregation fire him was no man! A rabbi's task is to shake the status quo, to raise religious consciousness and observance, to correct errors, to combat endocratic surplus. To do these things necessarily entails causing some unhappiness and dissatisfaction in the community—sometimes to the point where the rabbi endangers his job. But the rabbi needs to be able to rock the boat while at the same time avoiding a mutiny. Gevurah is an essential trait in this process.

In an essay in *Tradition*, Rabbi Joseph B. Soloveitchik stated that "heroism is the central category in practical Judaism," and further, that the adherent of halakhah must have the inner strength "which makes it possible for him to be different" (*Tradition* 17, no. 2, p. 13). Elsewhere, he wrote: "Halakhic man does not quiver before any man; he does not seek out compliments, nor does he require public approval. . . . He knows that the truth is a lamp unto his feet and the Halakhah a light unto his path" (*Halakhic Man*, p. 89). These expressions of the quality of Gevurah are deeply rooted in the Jewish tradition, going back to the time of Abraham. Indeed, Abraham is glorified in rabbinic literature for his ability to stand alone as a monotheist in a pagan world. It was as though Abraham were on one side and the rest of his society on the other side; and yet, Abraham did not back down. Rather, he strove to influence others to a belief in One God.

Religiously observant Jews have always been prepared to be at odds with the prevailing mores and values of the societies in which they lived. They have struggled heroically to maintain Shabbat, kashruth, family purity, modesty, holiness. A religious Jew knows existentially what it means to stand alone, to cling to one's own traditions and beliefs even in a society where most people follow a different pattern of living. One who would be a religious Jew must be a nonconformist!

Jewish heroism is manifested not only in the commitment to rituals and traditional observances, but also in the Jewish philosophy of life. In spite of all the tragedies that have befallen humanity in general and the Jewish people in particular, religious Jews maintain an unflinching optimism. Humanity will improve. Righteousness will prevail. The Messiah will bring redemption to the world. To propound this optimistic view of the human drama is an act of faith and courage. It seems to fly in the face of the lessons of history.

At the Hanukkah candle-lighting ceremony at New York's City Hall, convened by Mayor David Dinkins on December 21, 1992, I made the following comments:

Through all our generations, humanity has been locked in a painful and debilitating struggle between the forces of love, truth and peace on the one hand; and the forces of hatred, falsehood and violence on the other hand. And if we have learned anything at all from history, it is that good people do not always win. Indeed, the forces of good are often in the minority.

The holiday of Hanukkah reminds us of an eternal human lesson: one individual, a small group of individuals can make a difference. Hanukkah celebrates the victory of the few Israelites against their many oppressors; the victory of righteousness and love over wickedness and coercion. What guided these Jewish heroes of Israel and humanity was their trust in God, their deep sense of self-respect, and their unquenchable optimism that righteousness and truth can be vindicated if people are willing to make sacrifices. We can learn from them not to despair in the face of injustice and cruelty, not to lose heart though the cause of righteousness is defended only by a few of us, not to cringe even if our enemies appear more numerous and mightier than we are. On Hanukkah, we read in synagogue the words of the prophet Zekhariah: "Not by might and not by physical strength, but by My spirit, said the Lord of Hosts."

A rabbi must reinforce the spirit of heroism within his fellow Jews, reminding them of the grandeur of the Jewish tradition and the privilege of representing Torah to the world. He must stimulate them to work for the coming of the Messiah while at the same time teaching them to wait patiently for the ultimate redemption.

A rabbi, while devoted to a message of optimism, must strengthen himself to deal with failure and frustration.

Yes, the power of courage and heroism can achieve many wonderful results in the world. But good does not always prevail over evil; and good people do not always—or even usually—seem to win the battles of life. And the world has no shortage of immoral and amoral human beings.

The Torah commands us to love our neighbors as ourselves. This is a doable commandment when we are dealing with lovable, good people. But it is far more difficult when we are relating to people who are not very lovable, who are troublesome, even wicked. It takes considerable Gevurah to avoid disliking or despising some people.

During my career as a rabbi, I have dealt with many wonderful individuals. But I have also had to relate to people for whom I had little or no respect or affection. In rare cases, I have had to deal with individuals whom I would classify as being wicked—cruel, ruthless, malicious. They seemed to me to stem from the *sitra ahra,* the "other side," the fountain of evil. How could I bring myself to love them, when I did not even like them?

I have tried to draw strength from the talmudic account of Beruriah, the learned wife of Rabbi Meir. Beruriah taught that one should hate the sin, not the sinner. One should despise a wicked person's conduct and ideology, but not the person. Indeed, one can easily find grounds to pity the wicked person: he had a terrible upbringing, she was abused by her parents, he was rejected by his peers, she was scorned by others. The emotion of pity helps keep one from falling into hatred. Hatred is a self-destructive emotion that demeans and consumes the hater. When the Torah commands us to love others, it thereby teaches us to keep our own dignity and self-respect.

Thus far, we have discussed Gevurah in the context of having the courage of one's convictions, the inner strength to withstand external pressures, the heroism to live a holy and righteous life even in a profane and unjust society. But Gevurah is also a feature of the way one deals with suffering and misfortune. It is evident in the power to confront and overcome disappointments.

Viktor Frankl, the founder of the school of logotherapy, was a prisoner in one of the Nazi concentration camps. In these camps, innocent human beings were tortured and degraded, literally worked to death. The Nazis were fiendish in dehumanizing their victims, attempting to rob them of any vestige of human dignity. Frankl noted, though, that even in such a horrendous setting as a Nazi concentration camp, "it was possible for spiritual life to deepen." He observed that sensitive people "were able to retreat from their terrible surroundings to a life of inner riches and spiritual freedom." Frankl drew strength from Dostoevski's words: "There is only one thing that I dread: not to be worthy of my sufferings."

Suffering is part of human existence. We do not willingly invite it into our lives, but it arises all the same. People experience pain and discomfort due to natural causes: illness, harsh climatic conditions, famine. They suffer at the hands of other human beings, who abuse them physically, psychologically, emotionally. And they must deal with their own inner psychological anguish when they feel lonely, helpless, betrayed. The religious message does not deny the reality of suffering, but tries to help us cope with it in as heroic a way as we can. We can never fully answer the question: Why do we suffer? But we can deal with another question: Given that we suffer, how do we best respond to the challenge?

Rabbis are often involved with people who are undergoing suffering. Every rabbi has visited the ill, comforted the mourning, and counseled the distraught. As a young rabbi, I recall my anxieties about giving advice to those in pain. After all, what did I know of their inner feelings and thoughts? What advice could I give them, when they were the ones going through the suffering? But as the years passed, I came to realize that a rabbi—and any caregiver—can be helpful just by being there, by listening, by making a few thoughtful comments.

The fact is that we all learn and grow from our sufferings. We also have much to learn from those who are undergoing illness or grief. Those who handle their sufferings with Gevurah provide powerful models for their families and friends.

At times, Gevurah is manifested in courageous actions and words. At times, it is manifested in silent submission to the will of God. At all times, it is an essential characteristic for a rabbi, and for every person who strives to be genuinely religious.

7

Tiferet—Splendor, Glory

A story is told of a Jewish man who was riding on the subway, reading a Nazi newspaper. A friend of his, who happened to be riding in the same subway car, noticed this strange phenomenon. Angrily, he approached the newspaper reader: "Moshe, are you out of your mind? How can you be reading a Nazi newspaper?"

Moshe responded: "I used to read the Jewish newspapers, and what did I find? Jews being persecuted, Israel being attacked, Jews assimilating and intermarrying, Jewish poverty growing. It was too painful to read. So I switched to this paper. Now what do I find? Jews own all the banks. Jews control the media. Jews are all rich and powerful. Jews rule the world. The news is so much better! It's really a pleasure!"

It is true that Jewish "news" tends to focus on our many problems. It is also true that enemies of the Jews attribute to us exaggerated success and power in order to stir their discontented followers with resentment against Jews. In fact, no matter what newspaper a Jew reads, whether pro-Jewish or anti-Jewish, there is plenty to cause anxiety.

History has not been easy on the Jewish people. We have struggled with numerous internal problems in each generation. We have also waged an eternal battle against Amalek, the wicked forces of humanity that have striven to harm and destroy us. Since the days of antiquity through the present moment, Jews have been victims of hatred, dehumanization, and violence. The pages of Jewish history are filled with our many sufferings: exiles, expulsions, pogroms, libels, insults, legal disabilities, anti-Jewish propaganda, the Holocaust.

Jews are perplexed: Why has hatred been aimed at us? Why have we had to endure anti-Semitism, generation after generation? Our perplexity is intensified by the fact that we know ourselves to be good, constructive people. By and large, Jews are honest and hard-working. We strive not only to maintain ourselves and our families, but we make many positive contributions to the societies in which we live. From biblical times to the present, Jews have helped shape the civilization of the Western world to an incredible extent, far beyond what could have been expected from such a tiny nation.

Benjamin Disraeli, in his novel *Tancred*, captured the Jewish frustration with those who malign us, in spite of (or because of?) what we have given them. Eva Besso, one of the characters in the novel, says with emotion to a Christian visitor: "Persecute us! Why, if you believed what you profess, you should kneel to us. You raise statues to the hero who saves a country. We have saved the human race, and you persecute us for doing it." Later in the novel, Disraeli writes: "The life and property of England are protected by the laws of Sinai. The hard-working people of England are secured in every seven days a day of rest by the laws of Sinai. And yet they persecute the Jews and hold up to odium the race to whom they are indebted for the sublime legislation which alleviates the inevitable lot of the labouring multitude!" The Christian Tancred, the central character of the novel, comes to the conclusion that the inspired Hebrew mind has shaped the morality of the world. According to him, "Christianity is Judaism for the multitude, but still it is Judaism, and its development was the death-blow of the pagan idolatry." The continued Jewish influence through the Bible is immense; the most popular poet in England is King David, the great Jewish king.

In rabbinic tradition, Jews are known as "compassionate people children of compassionate people." Compassion and justice are our hallmarks. And yet, in each generation there are those who rise up against us, who persecute us, who threaten our security. And in each generation, we must speak out in defense of the outraged honor of the House of Israel.

The vocal and violent anti-Semites of the world do not hate us because of who we are, since they do not even know who we are. They have never bothered—nor do they want to bother—to understand us as individual human beings, to learn what we think, what we feel. They hate us without knowing us. We are hated, not for who we are, but for what we represent. The Jewish people, going back to Abraham and Sarah, have embodied profound teachings that make some people very uncomfortable.

Among the central (and revolutionary) notions that we have given to the world are the following: God created the universe, and all human beings are His subjects. All are answerable to Him for their deeds. Because God is King, human beings must live with humility and a profound sense of personal responsibility. Many people do not like this message. The tyrannical want to dethrone God. The irresponsible do not want to see themselves as answerable to God. But the Jewish people, by its very existence, constantly and quietly reminds the world that God is King, and that everyone is answerable to Him.

We have taught the world that God relates providentially to human history. Life has meaning, and it is a spiritual meaning. Our universal message rejects hedonism and materialism. And many people do not like this message. They are driven by hedonism and materialism. The Jewish teachings give them a guilt complex; our message challenges their warped values. So they lash out against us.

We have emphasized that humanity will ultimately be redeemed. A time will come when peace and respect will prevail, when the people of the world will recognize the One God who created all of us. The messianic era will be characterized by tolerance and understanding. National, religious, and ethnic rivalries will give way to a sense of universal harmony under the rule of God. But much of humanity seems to reject this vision. They prefer violence and wars; they deny the national, spiritual, and cultural legitimacy of others. The forces of hatred are powerful and widespread.

I think that the Jews are the conscience of the world. Many people would prefer not to be bothered by a conscience that reminds them of ideals and responsibilities. Many seem to be annoyed that the Jews have been able to maintain these lofty ideals century after century, for thousands of years. Some are jealous of our message; some are resentful of it; some despise it. So they attack individual Jews and Jewish institutions. They do so not because they have anything in particular against those Jews and those institutions, but rather because they view the Jews as symbols of ideals and principles. The Jewish message negates their violent or unethical or materialistic way of life.

Many Jews carry Jewish identity but do not understand it and do not live according to Jewish tradition. They, too, suffer from the attacks of anti-Semites, but do not necessarily comprehend why. They do not realize that they are symbols, willingly or unwillingly, of the Jewish view of life. On the other hand, Jews who live by the authentic teachings of Judaism are better able to withstand anti-Semitism with inner courage and understanding.

A positive Jewish response to anti-Semitism has been to build our communities to be even stronger and greater. In being true to our Jewishness, we are being true to ourselves and to the world. It is our noble responsibility to stand up for Jewish honor and principle, to work and struggle against bigotry and injustice; to make the world finally realize that the Jewish message is one of peace and fulfillment for all humanity.

In 1994, while our daughter Ronda was a student at Barnard College, a vicious anti-Semite, a leader of the Nation of Islam, was invited to speak on campus by a black student group. Enormous controversy ensued, but the speaker—as could have been expected—was allowed to preach his message of hatred. To assuage the pain and confusion among the student body, sessions were later arranged to address the issues of bigotry, anti-Semitism, hatred. I wrote an open letter to Ronda that was published in a number of Anglo-Jewish newspapers throughout the country. The following are excerpts from that letter:

The Passover Haggadah teaches that in every generation enemies arise to destroy us. And in every generation, that statement has proven true. Including this generation.

Perhaps those who are not Jewish do not have a real idea of what we have to face. We are a tiny people, a fraction of a percent of the world's population.

And yet, anti-Semites make the most outlandish charges and express the most vicious libels against us. When hate-mongers from the Nation of Islam blaspheme the Jewish people, they are cheered by their followers and defended by others as having the right to free expression. That their rhetoric of hatred impinges seriously on the freedom and well-being of Jews does not seem to get factored into the discusssion. When the news media consistently run stories biased against Israel, when they give a forum to Holocaust deniers and other bigots, when they publicize the hateful words of Jew-baiters—then we know that our generation, too, faces deadly enemies. People don't seem to realize that the rhetoric of hatred leads to acts of violence, that the dehumanization of Jews is, in fact, only one visible symbol in the breakdown of society. How Jews are treated is the litmus test for a society.

For thousands of years our people have weathered the storms of persecution. In spite of the immoral hatred and violence perpetrated against us over the centuries and in many lands, the Jewish people are still here to tell our story. Our enemies always disappear; we always survive. That is an iron law of history. And that bothers the anti-Semites greatly.

I suppose we should feel complimented. The enemies are jealous of the incredible successes of the Jewish people. Our Bible is venerated by Christianity and Islam and has been a major influence for human civilization. For thousands of years, our heroes have been scholars and sages, people of piety and faith. Jews have distinguished themselves for their service to humanity far out of proportion to our numbers. Our enemies resent our persistent commitment to excellence.

Some hate us because they see in us a highly educated, highly idealistic, highly philanthropic group. In contrast to their much larger groups, we are an annoying paradigm. When they can't come to grips with their own shortcomings, they look for a scapegoat; and we are a convenient target since we are so small and yet so visible.

The truly remarkable thing is that Jews are eternally optimistic. We always believe that reason and benevolence will prevail. We always work as though we can make society better. We believe that even evil humans can be redeemed through love and compassion.

When Jews come under fire from anti-Semites, we can call on our collective historic memory to give us strength. Our people has survived the millennia due to incredible courage and fortitude. We are the children of the prophets who taught justice, righteousness, and love to the world. The generations of Jews before us did not give up on themselves or on others.

Be strong and of good courage. It is our turn to defend the dignity and honor of the Jewish people. To the anti-Semites we say: heal yourselves. And to ourselves we say: we are proud to carry the badge of the Jewish people.

The day will come when hatred and bigotry will disappear from humanity. In the meanwhile, stay strong, courageous and faithful to our tradition. And to our collective Jewish memory.

Moses told the Israelites to be faithful to the commandments of the Torah: "For this is your wisdom and your understanding in the sight of the peoples, that when they hear all these statutes shall say: Surely this great nation is a wise and understanding people" (Deuteronomy 4:6). The people of Israel, through their devotion to the laws of the Torah, will inspire the nations of the world to see the wisdom and profundity of the Torah's teachings. Those who scorn the Torah and the Jewish people display thereby their own spiritual weakness and hinder the ultimate redemption of humanity.

In the kabbalistic order of sefirot, the quality of Tiferet (splendor, glory) stands above Hesed (compassion) and Gevurah (heroism). By drawing on and harmonizing the internal characteristics of compassion and heroism, Tiferet manifests splendor, glory, and beauty. The Jewish people, in its relationship with the other nations of the world, is supposed to demonstrate Tiferet; it is expected to be a model of dignity and glory. Although large numbers of non-Jews are hostile or neutral to the Jewish experience, the Jewish people will ultimately succeed in conveying its message to the world. And, as people come to understand the teachings of Judaism, they will also appreciate the Tiferet that the people of Israel represent.

A rabbi, by choice or by communal expectation, is a spokesman for the honor of the House of Israel. He constantly reminds his fellow Jews of their role as a beacon of spiritual splendor and glory, of their responsibility toward humanity.

In various lectures and sermons that I have given over the years, I have referred to the fact that the Jews offered seventy sacrifices at the Temple services in ancient Jerusalem during the festival of Succoth. Early rabbinic tradition pointed out that these seventy sacrifices were offered by the Jewish people for the well-being of the seventy nations of the world. (The ancient rabbis held that humanity was composed of seventy nations.) "Just as the dove [offered at the Temple] atones for everyone, so Israel atones for all peoples. The seventy calves that were burned on the altar at the feast of Succoth were offered on behalf of the nations, in order that their existence might be maintained in this world" (Midrash Shir ha-Shirim 4:1).

The Talmud (Gittin 61a) notes that Jews are obligated to care for the poor and needy of the non-Jews, visiting their sick, burying their dead, and generally helping to create a harmonious society. In spite of the fact that Jews have suffered so much at the hands of non-Jews, the Jewish commitment to a righteous and compassionate society remains vital. We have not given up on humanity, even though humanity has often given up on us.

For ten years, beginning in the mid-1980s, our congregation was one of the Jewish groups that sponsored a homeless shelter in New York City. We housed ten men per night, Sunday through Thursday, from December through March. Nearly all of the homeless men we served were not Jewish. We offered them a safe, warm place to sleep; showers for washing up; food in the evening and morning. Dozens of members of our congregation participated as volunteers. Numerous others contributed winter clothing, food, and money. We also participated with the interfaith Partnership for the Homeless and with Beyond Shelter, a Jewish organization that works to provide long-term housing solutions for the homeless. In generating support for these projects among our congregants, I emphasized the Jewish responsibility to help all people, to alleviate pain and suffering, to be constructive citizens. Our congregants, who shared this philosophy, were magnanimous in their involvement.

Congregation Shearith Israel, founded in 1654, has a long history of communal involvement. We have always taken our civic responsibilities quite seriously and have been ready to provide help for those in need, regardless of their religious affiliations. Members of the congregation have held public offices, and have played leadership roles in the establishment of hospitals, schools and colleges, social service and philanthropic agencies. In my own rabbinic career, I have served on the boards of a variety of organizations, including the National Child Labor Committee, Cancer Care, the American Indian Ritual Object Repatriation Committee, and the HealthCare Chaplaincy. In 1992, I served on New York City's Columbus Quincentennial Committee, together with representatives of many other ethnic and religious groups. While serving as president of the Rabbinical Council of America (1990–92), I had occasion to represent our organization in a number of communal capacities, including a significant meeting with President George Bush on the topics of education and intergroup relations. In these and other settings, I have tried to represent Jewish values and ideals in the larger non-Jewish community.

A rabbi is called upon to participate in communal meetings, interfaith dialogues and discussions, media events, and organizational work. While the demands on one's time can be burdensome, time must nonetheless be made for these communal activities. On an idealistic level, this is in fulfillment of the Jewish sense of responsibility for society as a whole. On a pragmatic level, every such occasion offers the opportunity to give our non-Jewish associates a better understanding of Jews and Judaism.

Tiferet—Splendor, Glory

Since our congregation is so historic, we receive many visitors who come on tours of the synagogue. Over the years, many non-Jewish groups have participated in these tours and have deepened their awareness of the history of Jews in America. I have led some of these visiting groups, including groups of Christian theological students. I have also given a number of lectures and speeches to non-Jewish audiences. In these various contexts, I have received many questions about Jewish theology and practice. Often, the questions were based on ignorance or misinformation about things Jewish. Some of the memorable questions include: Why do Jews believe devils live in corners? (We don't! In fact, we don't even believe in devils.) Why haven't Jews served in the American military? (We have! And with much heroism and distinction. Members of our congregation, for example, have fought in America's wars, going back to the Revolution.) Why do Jews use the blood of non-Jews for ritual purposes? (We don't and never have. This is a malicious anti-Jewish canard known as the blood libel. It staggers the imagination that anyone could ever have believed such nonsense, and it is even more astounding that this issue could still be raised in our "enlightened" modern era.)

Regrettably, many non-Jews have little genuine knowledge of Jews and Judaism. They pick up anti-Jewish attitudes and beliefs in their homes, schools, and/or religious institutions. Anti-Jewishness is a clear example of endocratic surplus, the psychological process of losing one's autonomy by internalizing too much from external sources. The best antidote is to provide correct information to dispel the anti-Jewish stereotypes that have been passed down generation to generation. A rabbi (indeed, every knowledgeable Jew) has a responsibility to clarify misconceptions, to show the peoples of the world the Tiferet—the beauty and splendor—of the Jewish tradition.

During my rabbinic tenure, I have participated in many interfaith dialogues and discussions. I well recall the Jewish-Christian dialogue held at the Graymoor Ecumenical Institute in October 1980. Sponsored by the Anti-Defamation League of B'nai B'rith, the Lutheran Council of America, and the Graymoor Fathers, it brought together a group of Jews, Catholics, and Protestants for a two-day conference. The main speaker of the event was Rev. Dr. Clemens Thoma of Lucerne, Switzerland, who had written a book entitled *Towards a Christian Theology of Judaism*. The beautiful grounds and facility of Graymoor formed an ideal setting for thoughtful discussion and good fellowship. Aside from the satisfying program and the informal discussions among participants, I was moved by another unique experience.

While our group was eating its meals in the dining hall, the brothers of Graymoor, dressed in their cassocks, were also taking their meals. Looking at them, I could not help but remember that my ancestors had been among the victims of the Spanish Inquisition, and that my Jewish forebears in Spain had been expelled en masse by Ferdinand and Isabella in 1492. Among the great enemies of the Jewish people in those days were the Catholic clerics who fomented hatred against the Jews. And now, I was sitting comfortably as a respected guest in a monastery, in the fellowship of Catholic priests and brothers—and eating the strictly kosher meals which they had arranged for the Jewish participants. History had not stood still!

Shortly after the conference, I became involved in another project designed to create more understanding between Jews and Christians. Leon Klenicki and Geoffrey Wigoder invited me to contribute twelve essays to a volume they were editing: *A Dictionary of the Jewish-Christian Dialogue*. Published by the Paulist Press, the book appeared in 1984. It included essays on thirty-six topics, with a Christian and a Jewish writer dealing with each topic. My topics were: Afterlife, Church and Synagogue, Covenant, Creation, Dogma, Law—Halakhah, Messiah, Pharisees, Prayer, Repentance, Revelation, and Tradition. The book was an interesting attempt to show how Jews and Christians, each in their own way, understand certain key terms. Meaningful dialogue can take place only when the participants all have a shared understanding of one another's theological preconceptions.

During the 1980s, I regularly attended meetings of the West Side Clergy Association, composed of the various clergy people of our neighborhood. I was the only Orthodox rabbi to participate. The discussions generally focused on humanitarian issues as well as areas of interfaith cooperation. From time to time, questions arose relating to the State of Israel. Several of the Christian clergy did not fully understand the centrality of Israel to Jews living in the United States. One of them said: "Look, we have Christians living all over the world. I feel for all of them, but nothing as visceral as American Jews feel for Jews living in Israel." This comment provided the opportunity for clarifying to Christian clergy the unique characteristics of the Jewish people. We are not merely a religious group, although Judaism is a great world religion. We are also a peoplehood, a nation. The Bible describes us as the Children of Israel; that is to say, we are an extended family. Our homeland in antiquity was Israel, with Jerusalem as its capital. We were massacred and exiled by our enemies, first the Babylonians and then the Romans, and we had been stateless for nearly two thousand years until the establishment of the State of Israel in 1948. During all those centuries of exile, the Jewish people retained its sense of peoplehood; we have always said our prayers in the direction of Jerusalem; we have never given up the dream of returning to the land that God promised to us. During the many centuries of our long exile, most of Christendom and Islam was hostile to us, depriving us of elementary rights. Our generation of Jews has lived to witness the incredible rebirth of the Jewish people in our ancient homeland. Whether Jews are born in Israel or America or France or anywhere else, they cannot but feel a sense of amazement at the newly reestablished Jewish state. We worry day and night about the threats to its security; we are anxious about its economic, social, political, and spiritual life. It is a tiny country, fragile in spite of its strength. We want to see it grow and succeed.

The Christian clergy in our group came to understand why Israel is so important to Jews, and developed greater sensitivity in their own attitudes toward Israel. One of the values of interfaith discussions is that they enable all the participants to become more aware of one another's feelings and assumptions.

On February 3, 1992, I attended a meeting convened by Cardinal O'Connor along with about forty other members of the Jewish community. He discussed his recent trip to the Middle East and his concerns for the peace process among Israel and her Arab neighbors. He also discussed other humanitarian issues that were on his mind. In writing up my impressions of this meeting that night, I made the following observation:

One of the feelings I had at this meeting, as I have had at other interfaith gatherings, is that Christian clergy tend to speak in lofty terms, commiserating with the oppressed and downtrodden of the world. They express their mission to help all those in need, and portray a universalistic picture. On the other hand, we Jews are concerned with a much more elementary issue: our survival.

We Jews are such a small people and we face so many serious problems. While we certainly do worry about the well-being of humanity, and while we do our share—and more than our share—of philanthropy and social action, we must necessarily devote maximum effort and resources just to ensure Jewish survival. And if we are so intense in our concern for Israel, it is because it is so precious to us. It is the only Jewish country in the world. It is our "only child," upon whom our future rests.

With the increasing presence of Muslims in the United States, interfaith dialogues have sometimes expanded into trialogues. I participated in such a program in the mid-1990s at Princeton University. The conference included two representatives for each of the three faith communities—Judaism, Christianity, and Islam. The speakers, including me, were asked to focus on the basic ethical teachings of our religious tradition. The hope was that all who attended would gain insight into areas of common concern among the religions, and become more aware of those issues on which the religions had different perspectives. Several hundred people attended—and they were overwhelmingly from the Muslim community. It was a special feeling for me to be explaining Jewish religious ideas to a largely Muslim audience. The discussions that followed the formal presentations were characterized by respectfulness and a genuine interest in learning. The conference demonstrated that a congenial meeting of representatives of the three religions was possible. Differences in theological and political viewpoints did not mar the spirit of harmony.

In 1984, I participated in a program at the United Nations, in commemoration of the 850th anniversary of the birth of Moses Maimonides, the great Jewish philosopher and halakhist. A Christian Spaniard spoke of the relationship of Maimonides to Spain, the land of his birth. A Muslim speaker addressed the relationship of Maimonides to the Muslim world. After fleeing persecution in Spain with his family, Maimonides lived in Morocco briefly before settling in Egypt, where he served as court physician. My speech dealt with the central importance of Maimonides in Jewish intellectual life. I also discussed some of Maimonides' writings relating to the interrelationship of Jews and the nations of the world. While the presentations and subsequent discussions were not without controversy, the general tone of the event was positive. It was significant in and of itself that representatives of three faith communities had joined together for a public program in honor of a Jewish thinker.

On February 7, 1992, I met privately with Dr. Abdel Rahman Osman, imam of the impressive mosque on 96th Street and Third Avenue in New York City. A distinguished elderly gentleman, Dr. Osman was educated in Egypt. He was soft-spoken and cordial, a smile constantly on his face. He gave me an inscribed copy of the Koran, and I reciprocated by giving him an inscribed copy of *The Essential Pele Yoetz*, a book of Jewish ethics by Rabbi Eliezer Papo which I had translated into English. (I had learned in advance of his interest in ethical literature.) We had a lengthy discussion, each informing the other of elements in the religious beliefs and practices of his religious tradition. He emphasized Islam's teachings of peace and brotherhood; he also stressed that Islam and Judaism shared a common commitment to absolute monotheism, and that we were closer to each other than to Catholicism. I raised my concern that Islamic clerics were known to preach violence against Israel and Jews, and asked if he felt this tendency could be checked. He regretted the phenomenon, and said that he himself had no part of this kind of preaching. His message was one of peace and harmony.

On February 3, 1999, I met with Imam Izak El Pasha of the Masjid Shabazz in Harlem. He told me that he had been raised in Brooklyn as a Baptist. Conditions in his community had been difficult, with much poverty and even more frustration. Like many other young people, he had been attracted to the teachings of the Nation of Islam, the Black Muslims. Black pride more than theological considerations were what motivated him at the time. The Christian church taught that one should turn the other cheek after being slapped, but this philosophy had not proven helpful to the black community. He had been looking for an identification that would give direction and meaning to his life, and the Black Muslims seemed to be the right choice. They stressed black pride, self-help, personal virtue. But at the same time, the Black Muslim leaders preached anti-Semitism and hatred of whites in general.

The imam eventually came to reject the hate-filled aspects of the Nation of Islam, and moved into normative Muslim life. In his work at his mosque in Harlem, he teaches love of all people and emphatically rejects bigotry, whether on the part of whites or blacks. His publications reflect respect for Judaism and Christianity, and he constantly calls for tolerance and cooperation.

During May 1992, I traveled to South Dakota to spend five days with descendants of Black Elk, a Sioux holy man, whose teachings had been of interest to me. The president of our congregation, Alvin Deutsch, is an attorney and was then representing Chris Sergel, who had written a dramatic work based on the life and teachings of Black Elk. Learning of my interest in Black Elk from Alvin, Chris arranged for us to visit the Pine Ridge Reservation and meet with members of Black Elk's family. We climbed to the top of Harney's Peak, where Black Elk had received the vision that began him on his career as a holy man. We visited the fort where Crazy Horse was murdered. We gathered at the cemetery at Wounded Knee to pay our respects to the memory of those who were so brutally massacred in 1898. During this intense week, we learned much about the culture of Sioux Indians; and we also spoke to our hosts about teachings of the Jewish religion. Indeed, we found a number of areas in common: belief in one God, respect for nature, disdain for wastefulness, commitment to prayer and spirituality.

Since then, I have had occasion to meet and correspond with other American Indians, and to be involved in some activities on behalf of the interests of American Indians. I have learned much from these activities, and hope that I have also been able to convey Jewish teachings to this segment of the American population.

These are examples of my own interfaith discussions and activities. They reflect an aspect of the life of many American rabbis. As religious figures, it is natural for rabbis to be interested in the ways other people approach

God. It is also to be expected that rabbis have the desire to share their knowledge of Judaism with a broad spectrum of the population. Interfaith dialogues, aside from being innately fascinating, also serve the pragmatic goal of creating better intergroup understanding and cooperation.

But the rabbi's interactions with the non-Jewish community transcend interfaith dialogue and discussion. He also plays a role in civic and political life, in which he represents the interests and needs of the Jewish community. Some rabbis will devote more time to these sorts of activities, and some will devote less time to them. Yet, they are—and must be—a facet of the rabbi's communal responsibilities. Rabbis bring authentic Jewish learning and tradition into the larger non-Jewish society. They demonstrate the Tiferet—the splendor and glory—of the Jewish experience to the world at large, thereby sanctifying the Name of God.

8

Binah—Discernment

Some years ago, I was walking through the streets of Jerusalem on Tisha B'Av, the fast day commemorating the destruction of our ancient Temples. I pondered the talmudic passage that attributes the destruction of the Second Temple to the sin of *sinat ḥinam*, usually translated to mean "baseless hatred." It occurred to me that there is no such thing as baseless hatred! When people hate others, they generally posit a reason; it may not be a valid or sensible reason, but in their minds it is still a reason. Their hatred, as they see it, is not baseless at all. It is generated by some negative feature (real or imagined) ascribed to the victims of their hatred.

What, then, does the Talmud mean when it states that the Temple was destroyed due to *sinat ḥinam*?

It seems that the phrase needs to be understood in a different way. The word *ḥinam* should be translated as being derived from the word, *ḥen*, meaning "charm" or "grace." What the Talmud is saying is that the Temple was destroyed because people hated to see the charm and grace in others. They despised the *ḥen* of others.

We are, of course, commanded by the Torah to be loving and caring people. We are supposed to see the *ḥen* in our fellow Jews and fellow human beings. But it is easy enough to slip into an attitude of disdain or hatred. Instead of looking into another's eyes and seeing a fellow person, a tendency arises to dehumanize and stereotype the another. Barriers are created between us and them, between our group and their group. People stop seeing one another as fellow human beings deserving of respect, but as antagonists. They refuse to see the *ḥen*, the grace, in their perceived opponents.

When this corrosive process occurs within the Jewish people, we face the tragedy of *sinat ḥinam*. Members of opposing factions shut themselves off from their opponents. They speak against them, condemn them; they do not want to interact with them as members of the same people. This destructive behavior undermines the foundations of Jewish society and Jewish nationhood. It caused the destruction of our Temples in ancient Jerusalem, and continues to threaten our people in modern times.

There are those who stereotype and dehumanize Orthodox Jews and *ḥaredim*; who depersonalize Reform, Conservative, and Reconstructionist Jews; who despise religious Jews; who scorn secularist Jews. They are fast to see the flaws in those who do not share their viewpoint; and they are reluctant to see the *ḥen* in those they wish to discredit.

One result of this process is a breakdown in relationships. Different groups of Jews find themselves more and more among "their own kind," and artificial barriers separate Jews of one group from Jews of another. We stop seeing ourselves as one family with one overall mission.

The resultant infighting and disrespect do not lead to victory for any faction; on the contrary, they weaken the Jewish people as a whole.

In the kabbalistic scheme of sefirot, the level above Tiferet is known as Binah (discernment). Binah involves the power to draw distinctions, to separate one factor from another, to derive truth by logical deductions. Rather than focusing on a full, unified picture, Binah relates to each individual detail in its uniqueness. Binah copes with issues of diversity.

A rabbi, as a thinking Jew, requires the virtue of Binah when considering the unity of the Jewish people. Yes, we have always seen ourselves as a fundamentally unified body, the House of Israel, Kenesset Yisrael. But in fact we are segmented into a host of subgroups, each of which has its own specific characteristics. We need discernment to see each group on its own terms and to understand our relationship (or lack of relationship) with it. We need to see the ḥen of each individual, of each group—even when we may differ with them significantly.

One of the major areas of controversy in the Jewish community surrounds the concept known as pluralism. Most American Jews have a positive attitude toward this idea, especially as it relates to the role of Jews in the larger non-Jewish society. Pluralism implies that all religious groups should be tolerated, free to express their own beliefs and follow their own religious precepts. Non-pluralistic societies, in contrast, have been extremely dangerous for Jews and other minority religious groups. When the dominant group asserts that there is only one truth, only one valid approach to God, then it is just a short step to persecution and forced conversion of those who do not adhere to the dominant religion. This has been the historical experience in Christian and Muslim countries. Even when these countries exhibited tolerance toward minority religions, the level of tolerance was fairly low by modern standards. Jews, for example, were still subject to legal disabilities and social ostracism, not to mention economic and educational discrimination. So it is not surprising that Jews favor religious pluralism. This allows a dignified framework for their religious life, and removes the serious psychological scars caused by being considered an illegitimate minority.

But when it comes to the issue of pluralism within the Jewish world, controversy prevails. The Orthodox feel that they are the true adherents of the Torah tradition. If pluralism means accepting the validity of non-Orthodox movements, Orthodoxy necessarily must reject this concept. On the other hand, the non-Orthodox movements ardently promote pluralism as the means for attaining a harmonious Jewish community. They argue that all movements are equally legitimate expressions of Judaism, and that no one group has a monopoly on truth.

Since the 1980s, pluralism has been a battle cry among the non-Orthodox, and a red flag for the Orthodox. Relationships between these segments of the community are strained, almost to the breaking point. Emotions blaze, especially when discussing the state of religion in Israel, where the Orthodox rabbinic establishment sets the standards for religious life. The non-Orthodox deeply resent being marginalized by the Orthodox. The Orthodox deeply resent the non-Orthodox claim that all branches of Judaism should be granted the right to operate on equal terms. The Orthodox staunchly defend the traditional halakhic standards for marriage, divorce, and conversion; to allow each group to follow its own rules would inevitably lead to a dangerous fragmentation of the Jewish people. It is difficult to imagine a harmonious Jewish community when different groups use different rules for establishing Jewish identity and marital status.

The conflicts surrounding the issue of pluralism engage the time and emotional energy of most American rabbis, regardless of their denomination. Pluralism is not merely a bone of contention in local Jewish communities, but also pervades discussions on a national and international level in such organizations as the United Jewish Appeal–Federation of Jewish Philanthropies and the Jewish Agency.

In 1999 I wrote an essay entitled "Pluralism and Jewish Unity" that was distributed to major Orthodox Jewish organizations as well as to Jewish newspapers in North America. The following excerpts are from that article:

> In his essay, "The Pursuit of the Ideal," Sir Isaiah Berlin distinguishes between relativism and pluralism. Relativism is when we say: you have your preferences, I have my preferences, we have different tastes, and nothing more is to be said. When people assert that all movements have equal legitimacy, that all are true expressions of God's will—this is relativism. But pluralism, in the sense implied by Isaiah Berlin, is something different. It is when various individuals or groups may be fully convinced that they have the genuine (not relative) truth. Nevertheless, they still see value in other good, sincere and thoughtful people who have beliefs different from theirs. Pluralism, in this sense, does not ask anyone to compromise his or her basic principles and beliefs; rather, it allows them to hold fast to their faith while at the same time seeing positive value in others who do not share

their faith. If the proponents of pluralism would use the term strictly in these terms, the Orthodox (at least many of them) could accept it. But since it is generally used as a vague synonym for relativism, the Orthodox find it intellectually and religiously unacceptable. It turns out, then, that much of the controversy surrounding pluralism is based on a misuse of the term, where it reflects relativism rather than genuine pluralism.

Among the non-Orthodox, the Orthodox are sometimes branded as undemocratic, coercive, jealous for monopolistic power. But these claims miss the essential point: the Orthodox are not fighting for themselves. They already follow halakhic standards defining Jewishness and marital status. They will continue to be faithful to halakhah. The Orthodox are not contending for themselves, but for the unity of the entire Jewish people. They want all Jews to share one basic framework of standards for Jewish identity and marital status. This strategy is wise and progressive. Whereas pluralism/relativism unravels the wholeness of the Jewish people, halakhic standards will keep us as one people.

This is not to say that Orthodoxy has been successful in conveying its deep-felt commitments to the Jewish public. Religious extremism, especially directed against the non-Orthodox, has not been helpful in building bridges among the segments of the Jewish people. But we must not allow extremism, or extreme reactions to extremism, to shape the future course of Jewish life.

For the Jewish people to come together, we must get past catch-words and slogans. We must be able to rise above unpleasant personalities and inflammatory rhetoric. We need to see the issues for what they really are and to understand what is genuinely at risk. Let us be true to ourselves and our beliefs; and let us also be true to a vision of genuine harmony and wholeness for the Jewish people.

Pluralism/relativism is not the panacea which it is often purported to be. Quite to the contrary. It will undermine the basic unity of the Jewish people.

Throughout my rabbinic career, I have struggled with a serious inner conflict. On the one hand, I truly and thoroughly believe that Torah and halakhah are the basic components of Judaism; Orthodox Judaism alone is committed to the divine nature of Torah and halakhah. The other movements either reject or compromise these fundamental principles. Thus, I believe that Orthodoxy (as propounded by the modern Orthodox) is the proper expression of Judaism, and that other ideologies are deficient, even inauthentic, representations of classic Jewish religiosity.

On the other hand, my Orthodox beliefs themselves demand a commitment to Kenesset Yisrael, to the entire congregation of Israel. Even those Jews who reject my understanding of Torah and halakhah—they too are part of the people of Israel, and they too are to be loved and respected. In my estimation, very few of them should be categorized as wicked; many of them are misguided, or operate with different principles than I do. I genuinely like and respect many non-Orthodox Jews, and I have been impressed by their sincerity and integrity. On ideological grounds, we are opponents; on a personal level, we are friends. I think I can genuinely understand and appreciate some of their critiques of traditional Judaism, and even learn from them. A dynamic, living, modern Orthodoxy can be receptive to the insights of the non-

Orthodox while still remaining totally faithful to the age-old traditions of Torah life. Yet, when all is said and done, the non-Orthodox movements have veered away from traditional beliefs and patterns of Judaism, and are not committed to Torah and halakhah in the same sense that the Orthodox are. In sum, I reject the non-Orthodox ideology unequivocally, but I do not reject the non-Orthodox individuals.

Colleagues on the Orthodox right condemn my position as one of compromise and moral weakness. After all, if Orthodoxy purports to be the true expression of Judaism, then it should not only reject the non-Orthodox ideologies, but should also have no dealings with spokespersons of non-Orthodox movements. Inherent in this position is the assumption that dealing with non-Orthodox leaders is a de facto recognition of their religious legitimacy.

My response to the rejectionist position was included in an article I wrote for *Jewish Action* magazine (Fall 1996):

> The rejectionist position has a certain appeal within Orthodoxy. It seems a principled, uncompromising response to the deviations from halakhah of the non-Orthodox groups. Rejectionists have the satisfaction of believing that they stand for truth, that they have nothing to do with falsifiers of Jewish tradition. But the rejectionist position is seriously flawed. Its inflammatory rhetoric alienates non-Orthodox Jews from halakhic Judaism. It is prone to self-righteousness and a spirit of exclusionism, casting aspersions not only on non-Orthodox Jews, but on Orthodox Jews who support a conciliatory approach to the non-Orthodox. Rejectionism has failed to convince the non-Orthodox that the Torah way of life is one of kind-

ness, compassion, gentleness and sweetness. Worse, it has stimulated an ugly anti-Orthodox backlash. If the goal of halakhic Judaism is to win back the masses of Jews to respect halakhah, the rejectionist approach has proven to be an obstacle.

During the 1970s, when the issue of pluralism had not yet exploded in our faces, I worked with many rabbis, non-Orthodox as well as Orthodox, on the various committees of the Commission on Synagogue Relations of the New York Federation of Jewish Philanthropies. Looking back nostalgically, those were very good times. The spirit of idealism and communal concern eclipsed partisan antagonisms. We all worked together to build a better Jewish community, with little discussion of our theological and behavioral differences. Strong friendships emerged. Respect and affection prevailed among participants, regardless of their religious affiliations. For many years, the executive director of the commission was Rabbi Isaac Trainin, an Orthodox rabbi who was determined to keep denominationalism out of Jewish community life.

A similar spirit of idealism and cooperation was evident in other organizations in which I was active: the New York Board of Rabbis, the Rabbinic Cabinets of UJA, Israel Bonds, and Jewish National Fund, the Synagogue Council of America. We enjoyed pluralism in its true sense: each person holding his own beliefs, while recognizing goodness and kindness in others who held other beliefs. No theological legitimacy was requested or granted by anyone.

In 1998, I was awarded the Maria and Joel Finkle Prize by the New York Board of Rabbis. The award was established to recognize rabbis who strive to maintain harmony among the various movements of the Jewish community. It was presented to me by a long-standing friend, Rabbi Sheldon Zimmerman. We had first met in the early 1970s at a meeting of the Commission on Synagogue Relations of the Federation of Jewish Philanthropies. He was then serving as rabbi of Central Synagogue, a leading Reform congregation in New York. In 1998, when he presented the award to me, he was president of the Hebrew Union College–Jewish Institute of Religion, the rabbinical school of the Reform movement. The awards ceremony was itself a testimony to the notion that friendship and respect can exist among individuals with different religious perspectives.

When people know and like one other, when they enjoy cordial relationships, they are more apt to maintain civility when they disagree. Much of the vitriol in contemporary Jewish squabbling is exacerbated by the fact that the opponents often do not know or understand each other. When people genuinely respect one another, they will seek ways to avoid or soften controversy.

When I was president of the Rabbinical Council of America, I convened a number of meetings involving members of the RCA and members of the Conservative and Reform rabbinical groups. Some of the meetings were constructive; some were less so. But all served the goal of keeping respectful dialogue open among the rabbis of the three movements. This has been a commitment of mine since my early days in the rabbinate, and continues to be of importance to me.

Nonetheless, I admit that it has become far more difficult to maintain this position. First, the Orthodox community has moved more to the right, and sees little or no need to interact with the non-Orthodox. On the contrary, Orthodox isolationism is on the upturn. Many Orthodox rabbis feel communal pressure to distance themselves from interdenominational Jewish activities, especially on the rabbinic level. Moreover, the non-Orthodox have changed. They have made decisions that deepen the chasm between themselves and Orthodoxy. Reform has changed the definition of a Jew to include persons born of a non-Jewish mother and a Jewish father, a sharp break with halakhah. Many Reform rabbis participate in interfaith marriages, something abhorrent to religious traditionalists. The Reform movement will now ordain rabbis who are avowed homosexuals, a policy that violates Torah tradition. While the Reform movement has always rejected the binding nature of halakhah, the Conservative movement, which claims allegiance to Jewish law, has made decisions that violate the Orthodox understanding of halakhah, such as permitting driving to synagogue on the Sabbath, ordaining women rabbis, and fostering egalitarianism in synagogue services. In aligning themselves with the Reform on the pluralism issue, the Conservative have deepened the rift between themselves and the Orthodox.

In the above-mentioned article in *Jewish Action*, I expressed my concern:

> Although my sympathies are clearly with the conciliatory approach, I believe that it has not achieved enough. Moreover, I think the future will find this approach increasingly futile. The non-Orthodox movements have created serious, probably unbridgeable, rifts in the Jewish community. The time will come—it may already be here—when no serious Orthodox rabbi will feel comfortable participating in a "mixed" board of rabbis. To do so will mean sitting at the table with rabbis who not only

violate Shabbat and kashruth, but who perform intermarriages; who may not even be Jewish by halakhic standards; and who may be proud homosexuals. Moreover, the increasing belligerency of the non-Orthodox leadership on the issue of pluralism (i.e. the overt demand for legitimization of non-Orthodox movements) makes it uncomfortable, if not impossible, for responsible Orthodox leadership to continue to sit with them.

Still, in spite of the growing chasm between the Orthodox and the non-Orthodox, I think it is essential to keep struggling to hold the community together as best as we can. This can only be achieved with Binah, the discernment to recognize differences, to see the *ḥen* even in those with whom we disagree. We must understand people where they are, not where we think they should be. We must be ready to enter into serious dialogue, a process that involves listening carefully to others. We need to talk with one another, not at one another. These discussions will best take place among friends and acquaintances and within the context of Jewish communal organizations. I think that "mixed" boards of rabbis will play a decreasing role in this process.

Rabbis have the ultimate responsibility of setting the moral tone of discussion for the community. They need to articulate the differences that divide the Jewish community; but they also need to stress the areas of commonality. They need to foster a spirit of respectfulness, and set the example by their own words and deeds.

In the fall of 1997, I wrote an article with Rabbi Sheldon Zimmerman; it was published in numerous Jewish newspapers. The following is the text of the article:

More than twenty-five years ago, we first met at a meeting of the Federation of Jewish Philanthropies of New York. During the ensuing years, we served together on various committees—working to help Jews in need, striving to strengthen the cohesiveness of our community, drawing on shared ideals to make our world a better place.

We are a Reform rabbi and an Orthodox rabbi—and we were, and continue to be, good friends. We found, and still find, that we share many ideals, that we can work together respectfully and sympathetically. Our friendship continues to be a valued part of our lives.

As an Orthodox rabbi and a Reform rabbi, we have our differences. Orthodoxy and Reform have very different views on the nature of Torah, mitzvot, halakhah. These differences are deeply held on both sides. The gap between us in these areas is not bridgeable.

And yet, we are friends; we work together; we believe all Jews should be working together in a shared direction. Whatever one's religious perspective, each Jew is part of the historic people of Israel. We share a common past and a singular destiny.

We, along with a great many thoughtful and sincere Jews, are deeply concerned by the increasing polarization within our community. We are pained by the public confrontations in Israel, as we are anguished by inflammatory rhetoric in the United States.

Yes, we have strong disagreements. Yes, we want to ensure that our viewpoints are heard. Yes, we want our views to prevail. But no, the way to deal with each other is not through confrontation.

Rabbi Joseph Soloveitchik taught that the Jewish people are bound by a covenant of destiny. As children of

Israel, we are connected to each other by familial ties. Family members do not always agree and do not always get along—but they are still family.

While we argue about definitions of Jewishness, the outside world has little difficulty knowing who is a Jew: anti-Semites and enemies of Israel put us all together in the same basket. They do not care about theological distinctions among ourselves.

As Jews, whatever our religious views, we are members of a distinct and distinctive people. Sometimes family members become angry at each other, and sometimes they even become estranged. The only way to effect healing is for family members to rise above their differences, to overlook insults (real or imagined), to sit down together again in a spirit of reunion. By seeing each other as partners in a shared destiny rather than as combatants, family members can begin to grow closer and regain trust in each other.

We, a Reform rabbi and an Orthodox rabbi, want the Jewish family to come back together. We want Jews of all backgrounds to spend more time with each other in a spirit of working together, not at odds. We need to understand each other's deepest feelings and concerns. Recognizing that there are areas of difference which may never be resolved, we cannot let these differences paralyze us or cause us to attack or insult each other. We would be glad if all Jews would back away from destructive confrontations. Instead, we should all be seeking ways, quietly, calmly and in a spirit of mutual respect and friendship, to bring our people together.

We should not be seeking hollow "victories," if the result of these "victories" is to deepen the fragmentation of the Jewish people. It takes wisdom and moral courage to back off from hostile and self-destructive confrontation. It takes true greatness to have the strength to stand back from the precipice, to have a larger vision of what is at stake.

We, an Orthodox rabbi and a Reform rabbi, have a longstanding friendship based on our shared commitments as human beings and as Jews. We believe that almost all Jews share these commitments and should focus on them. We believe that the responsibility of Jewish leadership, and of the community as a whole, is to create a climate of respectful and calm dialogue among all of us. We ask that Jews here and in Israel take the long view of our peoplehood and not engage in destructive confrontation. We need to work together, to build a future together, to retain our sense of family togetherness.

We believe that almost all Jews share this vision. It is time, then, for Jews to work together for a cohesive and respectful Jewish community. Let us talk with each other, let us embrace each other as family.

And let us create the framework for the future peace and happiness of the Jewish people.

The quality of Binah, discernment, is needed when we consider the vast diversity of the Jewish people. Over the centuries, Jews have lived in many lands, have spoken numerous languages, have developed different cultural patterns and customs. The Jewish people is not one monolithic group. Our great diversity is actually a source of strength, although it sometimes has led to conflict. The following remarks, which were part of my acceptance speech upon being elected president of the Rabbinical Council (June 1990), illustrate this point:

> A little over eighty years ago, a Sephardic teenager from Turkey arrived in Seattle, Washington. He and sev-

eral other Sephardic newcomers had gone to the Ashkenazic Orthodox synagogue in order to connect themselves with the city's Jewish community. But the Ashkenazim had difficulty recognizing the Sephardim as Jews. The newcomers spoke Judeo-Spanish, not Yiddish; they had "strange" names like Alhadeff, Policar, Romey; they read Hebrew in an "incomprehensible" manner. Even when the Sephardim showed their tallitot and tefillin, the Ashkenazim were not altogether convinced of their Jewishness. Ultimately, a letter was sent from the Spanish and Portuguese Synagogue in New York testifying that those young Sephardim were really Jewish—and that seems to have clarified matters for the most part.

Yet, this was a painful episode in the lives of the young Sephardic Jews from Turkey and the Island of Rhodes. The Sephardic teenager I mentioned earlier was my maternal grandfather, Marco Romey, and he never forgot how his Jewishness had been questioned. He lamented the fact that historical circumstances had created such a deep rift between Sephardim and Ashkenazim that one group hardly could recognize its kinship with the other.

Now, two generations later, the grandson of that Sephardic immigrant in Seattle has been elected President of the Rabbinical Council of America! My grandfather would have been proud to witness this moment. The Jewish people has made great strides in healing the rifts among us.

Growing up as a Sephardic Jew, I learned quickly that the dominant Ashkenazic community had little knowledge of or concern with Sephardic culture. In the Jewish day school in Seattle, we learned Jewish customs and traditions almost exclusively from an Ashkenazic point of view. Sephardic history, rituals, holiday observances, foods, music, intellectual life—all were consistently ignored. It was as though Sephardim had no past and no civilization worth discussing. I don't believe that the teachers taught this way from malice; but simply from ignorance. The Sephardic tradition was of no interest to them. They taught Judaism as they themselves had learned it, without taking into consideration that other good and pious Jews had traditions of their own.

I never saw or ate chopped liver, gefilte fish, cholent, or kugel until I enrolled as a student in Yeshiva College in the fall of 1963. When these foods were served on my first Shabbat at Yeshiva, I asked classmates what they were. They looked at me incredulously: was I really Jewish? How was it possible for a Jew, let alone a religious Jew, not to know what these basic Sabbath foods were? I explained to them that I was Sephardic and that we ate different foods in honor of the Sabbath. They could hardly believe this.

A number of my Yiddish-speaking teachers consistently referred to me as Engel. Angel, a fine Sephardic name, did not sound Jewish to them, whereas Engel, a fine Ashkenazic name, did. Most Judaic studies teachers taught laws and customs exclusively from the Ashkenazic perspective. (Yeshiva did institute a Sephardic program under the leadership of Haham Solomon Gaon, thereby making it possible for students to become somewhat familiar with Sephardic halakhic traditions.) A number of people, upon learning that I was Sephardic, commented that they thought Sephardic life had come to an end with the expulsion of Jews from Spain in 1492. That Sephardim had continued to flourish throughout the Ottoman Empire, the Middle East, North Africa, and Western Europe seems not to have made an indentation in their consciousnesses. That Sephardim had been the pioneers of Jewish life in the New World also went relatively unnoticed and unappreciated.

In 1971, I wrote an article on Sephardic culture in America for *Jewish Life* magazine. The following is an excerpt from that article:

> The forces of Americanization have nearly destroyed Judeo-Spanish among the new generations. Therefore, the language which bound Sephardim together as Jews for nearly five centuries no longer unites young American Sephardim. With the language, much of the folklore has fallen into obscurity. Celebrations and religious observances have tended to assume an American air. The secularism of American civilization has lessened general religious observance among Sephardim. Americanization and secularization, though, are problems all Jews must face. The particular difficulty the Sephardim have in preserving their culture, however, stems from the fact that Jewishness in America is set by an Ashkenazic standard. The Sephardi's customs and attitudes, history and people are ignored. Sephardim are expected to be Ashkenazim if they want to be recognized as Jews, especially as Orthodox Jews.
>
> The Ashkenazication process is clearly evident, for example, in the day schools and yeshivot. Sephardic students quickly learn to use Yiddish words, to dress and to think like the other students. Sephardic history and culture are seldom if ever taught. Most Sephardic students, let alone Ashkenazic students, know practically nothing of post-1492 Sephardic history. The yeshivot hardly ever mention the names and works of the great Sephardic rabbis of recent centuries.

People are the products of their culture. In each individual's mind are the latent voices, dreams and visions of generations of ancestors. Sometimes when he least expects it, a voice from his past will emerge. He may see something, or hear something, or do something that will give him a profound sense of nostalgia, that will let him penetrate into his past. Without this dimension in human experience, he is deprived of something sacred. To ignore or to suppress Sephardic culture is to deracinate the Sephardim. As their Sephardic roots are weakened, so ultimately will their Jewish roots wither.

The article referred primarily to the situation of Sephardim of Judeo-Spanish background. But the basic points are true for Sephardim of Judeo-Arabic, Judeo-Greek, and other Sephardic traditions. Each group has—and is entitled to have—its own specific history and culture. While no one can be expected to be an expert on all the diverse groups of the Jewish world, everyone should be open to the diversity among our people. Simple intellectual curiosity should make us want to know about other groups of Jews. We are enriched by the contributions of all segments of the Jewish people to the spiritual treasury of Judaism.

Binah entails discernment of uniqueness, distinctiveness. It requires focusing on details and maintaining an attitude of intellectual receptivity. Binah opposes smugness and staleness. It challenges us to be intellectually alive.

Much of my career as a Sephardic rabbi has been devoted to studying and teaching about the Sephardic experience. My goal has been to inculcate Sephardic traditions among Sephardim, as well as to make the larger

Ashkenazic community aware of the Sephardic component of the Jewish people. In the fall of 1978, I founded Sephardic House with the encouragement of several Sephardic laymen. It was based at Shearith Israel under my leadership. As it grew into a national organization, Sephardic House moved into its own offices with its own executive director, currently Dr. Janice Ovadiah. I have continued to serve actively as honorary president. Sephardic House has been involved in promoting Sephardic culture through classes, lectures, film festivals, concerts, and publications. It has become an important cultural resource and center for information about Sephardic life.

In an article written for Jewish educators (*Ten Da'at*, Fall 1988), I noted:

> In order to teach the wholeness of the Jewish people, we need to have a broad knowledge and vision of the Jewish people. We cannot limit ourselves to sources only from Europe, just as we cannot limit ourselves to sources only from Asia or Africa. . . . There is more to a Jewish community than a set of interesting customs or folkways. We need to be able to speak of the Jews of Vilna and of Istanbul and of Berlin and of Tangiers with the same degree of naturalness, with no change in the inflection of our voices. We need to see Jews of all these—and all the other—communities as though they are part of "our" community.

One of the basic responsibilities of rabbis is to nourish a spirit of unity and understanding within a Jewish community that is diverse and segmented. Good rabbis lose sleep trying to cope with this duty.

9

Ḥokhmah—Wisdom

Dr. Meir Benayahu, in his book *Marbitz Torah*, discusses the various titles given to rabbis in Sephardic communities. His researches revealed that the prevalent appellation was the Hebrew phrase *marbitz Torah*, meaning "disseminator of Torah."

As this title indicates, the rabbi's chief function was to teach Torah and to conduct his congregation and community according to the laws of the Torah. Indeed, this has been the central responsibility of rabbis since antiquity. In Hebrew, the word "rabbi" means teacher.

Rabbis, like all true teachers, must constantly renew themselves through study and contemplation. They must always seek to improve their communication and pedagogic methods. Teaching Torah involves transmitting a way of life, a worldview. It demands outstanding talent, commitment, and patience. No rabbi is totally successful. Even so masterful a teacher as the late Rabbi Joseph B. Soloveitchik noted in a lecture given in March 1974: "As a teacher I can transmit my ideas to my pupils on an intellectual level. When it comes to the transmission and passing of experiences I feel so inadequate. Sometimes it drives me to despair" (Quoted from Aaron Rakeffet-Rothkoff, ed., *The Rav: The World of Rabbi Joseph B. Soloveitchik*, Hoboken, N.J.: Ktav Publishing House, 1999, vol. 2, p. 238). The rabbi is called upon not merely to convey a body of knowledge, but also to impart religious feeling, sensitivity, faith.

The modern American rabbi, as a *marbitz Torah*, finds himself giving classes, lectures, sermons, seminars. He spends many hours preparing his own talks, and also devotes much time to developing adult education programs involving guest teachers. He will gear his educational work to the broad spectrum of his congregation, giving advanced, intermediate, and beginners classes—depending on the level of Jewish knowledge of congregants. The Jewish education of the youth of his congregation is a matter of deep concern to him and may involve him both in a supervisory and a teaching capacity.

While many rabbis are "general practitioners," others have expertise in specific areas of Jewish learning. They are invited to give lectures and classes in other congregations and communities, as well as at conferences and conventions. They may also participate in educational programming on radio, television, and the Internet. Some of them devote time to research and writing, thus finding additional audiences through their publications. A growing number of congregational rabbis also devote time to teaching in local day schools, yeshivot, or colleges. A congregation that encourages its rabbi to study and teach helps the rabbi to grow as a *marbitz Torah*.

Sometimes rabbinical colleagues tell me that members of their congregations have complaints. They feel that the rabbi is devoting too much time to study and teaching;

instead he should be primarily involved in pastoral work, counseling, synagogue administration. Rabbinical school is over, they say; now it's time to work! While it goes without saying that a rabbi must meet the needs of his congregation, it also should be obvious that he cannot do so unless he constantly renews and deepens his Torah knowledge. He was not engaged by the congregation to be a social worker or administrator: he was appointed as rabbi. And a rabbi must be steeped in Torah if he is to be authentic. A rabbi must be able to manage his time in such a way that he can fulfill his pastoral duties while also maintaining a fixed time for Torah scholarship.

I have had the good fortune to be associated with a congregation that fosters research and writing by its rabbi. Two of my predecessors, Dr. Henry Pereira Mendes (who served Shearith Israel from 1877 to 1937) and Dr. David de Sola Pool (who served from 1907 to 1970) were prolific authors and made important contributions to Jewish scholarship. My own research and writing have been stimulated by the example they set. I have found that the books and articles I have written have helped me to clarify questions, deepen my understanding, share my discoveries with readers. I try always to be engaged in a research project. This helps me to structure my days so that I can devote time to Torah study; it keeps my mind focused on the subject I am working on; and it produces knowledge that can be shared in sermons, classes, discussions, and conversations. It seems to me that if a rabbi is not involved in intellectual struggles and challenges, he runs the risk of spiritual atrophy. Torah study is not a luxury; it is an absolute necessity.

Another title used for rabbis among Sephardim was *haver ha-ir*. The term *haver* generally refers to a person of distinction and learning, but it also has the connotation of "friend." Thus, the rabbi is seen to be a "friend of the city," a person who exercises leadership in a congenial manner. To communicate Torah teachings and values, it is desirable for the rabbi to be an approachable, likeable person. He thereby wins the confidence and goodwill of the public, and people become more receptive to his message. The rabbi should communicate by his demeanor that he shares the destiny of his congregation, that he identifies with them and cares deeply for their well-being.

In the summer of 1968, my wife and I visited Istanbul, and there we met an extraordinary rabbi who reflected the notion of ḥaver ha-ir. His name was Nissim Behar. He had a business in which he worked several hours a day. The rest of the time he devoted—without charge—to the Jewish community. He taught many students, and trained a number of young men who went on to become rabbis and teachers themselves.

Rabbi Behar invited Gilda and me to join him for Shabbat lunch. We were honored to accept. On the Friday morning before that Shabbat, we asked if we could assist with the preparations. He told us we could help him with the shopping. We were delighted. Rabbi Behar went to the market, bought a few vegetables, and gave me the sack to carry. We then went down the road to another market where he bought some fruit, and I received another bag to carry. Then we stopped at a third, fourth, and fifth store where he bought a few more small items. I asked: "Rabbi Behar, why are we stopping at so many stores? Why didn't you simply buy everything at the first store? That would have saved us a lot of time and trouble." He answered with great sincerity: "All of the storekeepers we visited are members of our community. They all have to earn a living. They have families to support. So I shop at each of their stores in order to give each of them some business and to wish them a peaceful Shabbat. They enjoy seeing me almost as much as I enjoy seeing them." Rabbi Behar's words have stayed in my mind as a profound example of a rabbi as *haver ha-ir*.

A third title that Sephardim used to designate a rabbi was *hakham*, sage. The *hakham*, of course, was expected to be a scholar and a paradigm of righteousness. But he was also expected to be wise in the ways of the world. He needed to understand human nature and human psychology.

The quintessential *hakham* is a man who is highly sensitive to the feelings of others. He listens carefully to their words, he observes their expressions and movements, he feels their joys and sorrows. He somehow is able to comprehend their deepest feelings and aspirations: he understands them.

A young rabbi may be very learned and enthusiastic, but he needs years of experience to attain the wisdom associated with the term *hakham*. This quality is gained not by teaching others, but by learning from others. As the Ethics of the Fathers teaches: "Who is a *hakham*? One who learns from everyone."

Sometimes, rabbis have difficulty learning this lesson. They believe they must present themselves as bastions of wisdom. Moreover, congregants may give the impression that they expect their rabbi to be a wise man. Thus, the rabbi is reluctant to show his own ignorance and vulnerability; he sees himself as the one who is supposed to teach others, not as an individual who must learn from all.

I remember an incident that happened to me when I had just begun serving our congregation as a student rabbi. I had given a rousing sermon of which I was quite proud. One of the elders of the congregation, though, did not share my enthusiasm for the sermon. He accosted me at the kiddush following services and proceeded to criticize me in very sharp language. I was infuriated by his presumptuousness. After all, I was far more learned than he; he owed me respect, since I was serving in a rabbinical capacity. At the conclusion of the Sabbath, I called the president of the congregation, Mr. Edgar J. Nathan 3rd, and demanded that he chastise the man who had treated me with such disrespect. But instead of siding with me, Edgar told me I should call the elder and invite him out for a cup of coffee. I was stunned. Why should I demean myself by calling this person? Why should I have to invite him anywhere? Why shouldn't I demand an apology? But Edgar insisted; and I agreed reluctantly to follow his advice.

The following Monday morning I called my critic and invited him out for a cup of coffee. A long silence ensued, after which the man said curtly: "Be in my office at noon." He then hung up the telephone. Now I was even more outraged. Who was he to speak with me so abruptly? But I swallowed my pride and went to his office at noon. When he opened the door, he embraced me and gave me a big smile. I could not have been more surprised by this reception. He proudly walked me around his office, showed me some memorabilia relating to his family's association with our congregation, and then took me out to lunch. He was a lively conversationalist, and filled me in on a lot of synagogue history. After all, I was just a new young rabbi; he was an elderly man, who had grown up in the congregation. He assumed the role of mentor, trying to help out a newcomer. By the end of the lunch, he actually praised the sermon I had given on Shabbat—the very sermon that had led him to criticize me in the first place!

When I returned to the synagogue office, I called Edgar and recounted what had occurred. I told him how amazed I was by the man's change in attitude toward me. Edgar, who had known the man for many years, told me that he had much to teach but was somewhat eccentric. He needed to feel needed. Once I had deferred to him by calling him up and inviting him out, he realized that I was interested in him, that I was reaching out to him. And that made all the difference. I thanked Edgar for an important lesson, one I have never forgotten. Doesn't everyone— eccentric or otherwise—need to feel needed? Doesn't everyone appreciate feeling important, serving as a mentor? Over the years, I have had many cups of coffee with a great many people—and I have always come away having learned something worthwhile.

I learned another valuable lesson from another event early in my rabbinic career. I was invited to attend a luncheon by a women's charitable organization, many of whose members were also members of our congregation. I was twenty-five years old, and not terribly eager to spend an afternoon with a group of women, many of whom were elderly, at a long-drawn-out luncheon. What a waste of time, I thought. But duty called, and I felt I had to attend.

But I certainly did not enjoy the event. I felt awkward as one of the few men there, and by far the youngest. I did not know what to talk about with the women; I was not much interested in being a conversationalist. I suffered through several hours, and then made my escape at the earliest appropriate time. I was angry. I had wasted several hours in an unpleasant setting. Rabbis should not have to do this. People should understand that a rabbi has better things to do with his time than attend luncheons and make small talk.

Soon after, I met with Haham Dr. Solomon Gaon, who had been my teacher at Yeshiva University and who continued to be a mentor as I began my career as a rabbi. I complained bitterly, and asked him to intercede on my behalf with the synagogue's Board of Trustees, telling them not to expect me to attend luncheons and social events. Haham Gaon, though, was not at all sympathetic. On the contrary, he said that I needed to learn to be more loving, caring, and thoughtful of others, and not to be so self-absorbed in my own projects. These women, he said, had gathered together at their luncheon for charitable purposes. They were all sacrificing time and money to help the community. They had been respectful enough to invite rabbis of the various congregations, including me. Few of the women had met me as yet, since I was still very new in the community. Wouldn't they have been delighted if the new young rabbi had greeted them warmly, congratulated them on their work? Wouldn't it have made their day if I had reached out to them with kindness and genuine interest? The Almighty had given me the opportunity to meet some wonderful people; He had given me the opportunity of establishing warm relationships with them. And what had I done? I had grumbled and growled and complained. I had lost an important occasion to be a rabbi, to learn from others, to share with others.

Haham Gaon's words astounded me. He was right! I had been wrong, self-centered, self-righteous. A rabbi is supposed to serve the public and bring them closer to the teachings of Torah; but to accomplish this, a rabbi must live among the people and be sincerely interested in their welfare. He must know when to study Torah, and when to put his study into action.

This does not mean that the rabbi should be an actor, always smiling with a canned grin, always coming up with a bon mot. On the contrary, rabbis who behave in such a fashion strike me as hypocritical and empty. The need is not to pretend an interest in others, but truly and genuinely to relate to them. This requires considerable skill and effort—and wisdom.

In the kabbalistic scheme of sefirot, Ḥokhmah (wisdom) is parallel to Binah (discernment). Whereas Binah tilts toward the power of analysis and reason, Ḥokhmah reflects a deep, intuitive wisdom, a unifying vision. Neither of these qualities is fully attained by any human being; but thoughtful people are constantly striving to increase their mastery of them.

A rabbi needs Ḥokhmah when he studies and teaches, when he serves the community, when he interrelates with others. But real wisdom is elusive. It is generally lacking in those who think they have it!

A biblical passage states: *veha-ḥokhmah me-ayin timatsei* (Job 28:12), "Whence shall wisdom be found?" The kabbalists understand this phrase in accordance with a second definition of *me-ayin*: not "whence," but "from nothingness." Thus, the passage states: "Wisdom will be found in nothingness"; in other words, one attains wisdom only when he first reduces himself to nothingness. The obstacle to genuine wisdom is egocentricity. Filled with a sense of your own importance and influence, you lose sight of your essential nothingness. You cannot grow fully in wisdom because your own ego is blocking the way. But a person who seeks wisdom must follow the path of humility. He must see the nothingness within himself and contrast that with the everythingness of God. When one fully understands this contrast and integrates it into his personality, he is on the first step in the quest for Ḥokhmah.

The Torah includes an enigmatic law concerning the purification brought about through the ashes of a red heifer. If someone had become ritually defiled by contact with a dead body, the purification process included being sprinkled by a priest (*kohen*) with these ashes. The oddity of this law, though, is that the same ashes that served to purify the defiled person also served to defile the priest who sprinkled them. The ashes purified the impure, but defiled the pure.

I suggest the following interpretation. During this ritual, the priest might internalize feelings of self-importance. After all, the ritually defiled must come to him for assistance. They are dependent on his ministrations. Yet, the priest must retain his sense of humility. He is a servant of the Lord and is fulfilling a Torah commandment. He is not supposed to become haughty or even slightly self-satisfied that he is officiating at this purification ceremony. The Torah, thus, teaches that the priest becomes impure from his contact with the ashes of purification. This will humble him, and make him realize that he must sacrifice his own purity to purify others. At the conclusion of the ceremony, he cannot march away in triumph and self-satisfaction. He must now start coping with his own ritual defilement and the need to undergo a ritual of purification.

This lesson has special relevance to rabbis, who often find themselves serving as religious functionaries—whether at synagogue services or life-cycle ritual events. A rabbi might start thinking that he is indispensable, or at least highly important. People depend on his blessings and prayers and words of wisdom. But once a rabbi internalizes such thoughts, he gives nourishment to egotism. He may come to develop a pompous, self-assured manner; he may lose the sense of his own nothingness, and thereby move further and further away from genuine wisdom. A rabbi must keep in mind that his services as a religious functionary should stem from a feeling of religious responsibility, not from a wish for self-gratification. In some way, he must see himself as becoming ritually defiled, that is, he needs to focus on his own religious shortcomings and his own need for purification.

Rabbis, though, are only human. It is not unnatural for them to take pride and satisfaction in having given a good sermon or a meaningful eulogy, in having comforted the ill and mourning, in having given good counsel to those with problems. Of course, rabbis should constantly strive to do their best. Yet, even when they have reason to applaud their work, rabbis should keep in mind their many failings. By remembering their essential nothingness even at times when they are at their best, rabbis (and all thoughtful people) can maintain a healthy spiritual balance.

Rabbis are often called upon to engage in tedious, time-consuming administrative functions. They may have to write or edit the synagogue bulletin, call people to remind them to attend minyan, oversee synagogue mailings, schedule various events, and so on. Sometimes, a rabbi may look into the mirror and ask: Did I become a rabbi so that I could tend to all these mundane details? Shouldn't I only have to operate on the spiritual and intellectual levels? My answer is that a rabbi must serve his congregation to the best of his ability on all levels where he can or must make a contribution. If the synagogue is large enough to have an administrative staff, he is spared from many such duties. But if it is not, he must meet every challenge with a good spirit. It is not humiliating or beneath one's dignity to serve the Jewish people: it is a privilege. And if some duties seem too mundane, they may serve to remind the rabbi not to become spiritually aloof or self-centered. Some of the great rabbis of antiquity were not ashamed to be water carriers and sandal makers. By serving the Jewish people with humility, a rabbi—though he may sometimes feel frustrated—actually may deepen his religious sensitivities toward his fellow Jews. Rabbis should take their work seriously, but they should not take themselves overseriously.

Dr. Samuel Belkin, who was president of Yeshiva University from 1943 to 1975, once addressed a meeting of rabbis, reminding his colleagues of the necessity of remaining humble. This is a challenge, he said, because rabbis are accustomed to being treated with honor. They may come to see themselves as worthy of honor, and then may even come to feel insulted if the honor is not given appropriately. Rabbis need to keep in mind that they are shown honor not because of their own virtues, but because they represent the Torah.

Dr. Belkin told a story about a special dinner sponsored by Yeshiva University on the occasion of his tenth anniversary as president. The event was held in a major New York hotel and was very elegantly arranged. Dr. Belkin, who was by nature a quiet and reserved man, was not at all comfortable about being the guest of honor. He consented to it, though, because the dinner would be an excellent opportunity to highlight the achievements of Yeshiva to its supporters, and also to win some new contributors.

Ḥokhmah — Wisdom

During the program, Dr. Belkin was seated on the dais, facing the audience. He listened patiently to the many speeches praising his brilliant service to Yeshiva. He kept telling himself that all the praise showered on him was hyperbolic, that he did not deserve it, that he was only doing his job. But he noticed a tall, stately man sitting in the front row—a distinguished gentleman whom Dr. Belkin had never met before. Whenever Dr. Belkin was praised by one of the speakers, this gentleman clapped enthusiastically. Dr. Belkin thought to himself: perhaps, after all, I am important. If this distinguished man has come to the dinner as a token of honor to me, and if he applauds me so eagerly, I must have done something good to have deserved this gesture of respect. Dr. Belkin could feel his ego swelling.

After the program and dinner, Dr. Belkin walked among the guests and happened to find himself in the company of the distinguished man who had clapped for him so energetically during the program. Dr. Belkin reached out to shake the man's hand, but the man responded with an expression of puzzlement on his face. "Do I know you?" the gentleman asked Dr. Belkin. "My name is Belkin," the president of Yeshiva said diffidently.

"Are you the rabbi of a synagogue?"

"No."

"Are you a cantor?"

"No."

"Are you a shoḥet?"

"No."

The man scratched his head and walked away, apparently disappointed by the encounter.

In relating this story to the assembled rabbis, Dr. Belkin reminded us that honor is hollow, vanity is great, and the tendency to self-deception is omnipresent. Even when being applauded enthusiastically, one should keep in mind that the person who is clapping may not even know who you are! We must not allow ourselves to be beguiled by honor and public praise.

The rabbi's Ḥokhmah comes into play not only in keeping focused on his own nothingness but also in his relations with members of his congregation. I have heard rabbis use the term *baalabatim* (i.e., synagogue members) as though it were a bad word, as though the *baalabatim* were the enemy. This is sad, because the rabbi's lifework involves constant interaction with the members of his congregation.

Every congregation has its own dynamic, and no two rabbis find themselves in exactly comparable situations. However, certain general characteristics seem to be universal. Every congregation has a core (usually relatively small) of hard-working, dedicated members. They do much of the volunteer work, serve on the board and committees. They are the most active members. Congregations also have a relatively small core of major financial supporters; these people may or may not be in the category of active members, but the synagogue needs their contributions in order to maintain itself. Congregations have a group of members who attend services regularly; they may or may not be active in synagogue life outside of services; they may or may not be generous supporters of the congregation. Most congregations also have a group (hopefully small) of people who perpetually seem angry and disgruntled, inveterate complainers. A large group of members pay their dues, turn up at services from time to time, attend a lecture or class periodically; but they are generally not active in the congregation and do not wish to be involved too much.

The rabbi is rabbi to all of them. Whether a member is rich or poor, young or old, married or single, intelligent or dull, active or inactive, religiously observant or careless about personal religious practices—each of them has a claim on the rabbi's time, energy, and concern. Moreover, the rabbi has to be something of an orchestra leader, attempting to maintain harmony among the different segments of the congregation. Different individuals and factions have different ideas on what is best for the congregation. A rabbi needs to be sensitive to what the people are thinking and saying; and he must strive to foster a sense of unity even among people who may have sharply different opinions.

Congregations need not be riven by politics, but few rabbis can escape this phenomenon entirely. An elder member of my congregation once told me that dissension among members was a sign of vitality; it demonstrated that people cared passionately about the institution. If no one argued or disagreed or offered opinions, then this would be a sign of terrible apathy. This comment has some truth to it; but it is obvious that congregations function better without dissension. The rabbi, through his ongoing relationships with the members of the congregation, is often in the best position to keep things running smoothly. He can speak with all segments of the congregation, and can help shape a consensus among members in order to prevent major confrontations and disputes. Unless, of course, it is the rabbi himself who is the source of the dissension!

Unfortunately, there are always members who will give the rabbi a difficult time. Some are frustrated in their personal or professional lives, so the synagogue is a place for them to assert authority. They want to be noticed; they want to feel that they have control over the rabbi. Others have diverse negative character traits: they are complainers, or egomaniacs, or psychologically troubled in various ways. Some individuals complain that the rabbi did not visit them when they were ill, even though they never bothered to inform the rabbi of their illness. Somehow the rabbi is expected to know such things, to be something of a mind-reader.

Although I have been extraordinarily fortunate in my own rabbinic career, I have had to deal with a few members over the years who taxed my patience to the limit. Whenever they called, I immediately shuddered; I knew that they were calling with a complaint (usually unfounded). These individuals seemed never to have anything good to say, but only to look for faults and weaknesses. My wife told me, early in our rabbinic life: "When people like that call you, don't take it personally. Actually, you should feel sorry for them. You only have to deal with them for a few minutes, but they have to live with themselves day in and day out. What kind of lives can such people lead?"

A rabbi must not allow himself to be drawn into factionalism within the congregation. He needs to be a statesman who can bring wisdom and Torah values to the communal discussions. He needs to use his Ḥokhmah to help the congregation share a unified vision for the future.

The rabbi must know, as must anyone in public life, that it is not possible to please everyone. One must be sensitive to the needs and opinions of all members, but ultimately must make the decisions one believes will be best for the greatest number of congregants. A rabbi is not a contestant in a popularity contest. He is supposed to be a religious leader, guiding his congregation according to his best judgment. He will succeed more or he will succeed less; but he may never lose sight of his rabbinic mission.

Because the rabbi is a public personality, he is subject to criticism by his congregants and others in the community. There will always be those who will find fault with him, and who will express dissatisfaction privately or publicly. It is painful enough for the rabbi to deal with such criticisms; but it is even more painful for him if his family suffers from them. The rabbi chose a public career, knowing that controversy and criticism are inevitabilities. But the rabbi's family did not choose a public life; and yet, they suffer—usually in silence—when the rabbi comes under fire. The unsung heroes of a rabbi's career are his family members. Without their love, encouragement, and endurance, the rabbi could easily lose heart and become embittered.

The rabbi must constantly remind himself that he is serving a worthy goal. He must be prepared to face many challenges along the way. His vision should be grand and clear; it should transcend the everyday ups and downs of the rabbinate.

In a speech I delivered at the summer convention of the Rabbinical Council of America (June 1990), I shared with my colleagues some thoughts on the rabbi's role as a peacemaker. The following are excerpts from that address:

> Rabbi Elazar said in the name of Rabbi Hanina: "Rabbinic scholars increase peace in the world." Yet in what way do rabbis increase peace? (Indeed, it sometimes appears that rabbis are involved in altogether too much feuding and dissension!)

The answer may be found in Maharsha's commentary at the end of the tractates Berakhot and Yevamot. Maharsha tells us that rabbinic scholars bring peace between the people of Israel and their Father in Heaven. By teaching Torah, the prayers and blessings, the reverence and love of God—rabbis lead Jews to find peace in their relationship with God. When all is said and done, that is our ultimate responsibility.

Maharsha notes that our sages sometimes deviate from the technical letter of the law in order to bring peace among the Jewish people. They are guided by what is right in the eyes of God and humans. They try their utmost to generate and maintain harmony in society. They do not aim to be stringent or lenient; they aim at serving God and Israel in truth. Because of this attitude, they increase real peace among people. Rabbis must be known as peacemakers, not as troublemakers. People should see us as agents of harmony, not as agents of discord.

The Talmud (Pesahim 50a) relates the story of the seeming death of the son of Rabbi Yehoshua ben Levi. The son came back to life. Rabbi Yehoshua asked him: What did you see on the other side? He answered: I saw a topsy turvy world. The world there is an inversion of this world; those who are great here are small there; those who are small here are great there. Rabbi Yehoshua ben Levi responded: No, my son, the world you saw was not inverted at all, it was the real world, the clear reality. In this world, humans often misjudge who actually is great or insignificant, powerful or weak. But these misjudgments are rectified in the next world, the true world.

But then Rabbi Yehoshua asked his son: Where are we, the rabbinic scholars, in the next world? And the son responded: We are the same there as we are here. In other words, it is precisely the rabbinic scholars who see things as they really are, in their true clarity. The Torah gives us the ability to keep our eyes on what is real, to see through illusions.

We live in a world of noise, confusion and verbosity. There is so much commotion from so many directions that it becomes difficult to think quietly and clearly. Yet, that is the responsibility and challenge posed to rabbis—to think carefully, quietly, truly. We need to clarify what is important from that which is unimportant. We need to know when to speak and when to remain silent, when to act and when to refrain from action.

10

Keter—Crown

Several years ago, I received a call from a young woman who was planning a spring wedding. She wanted to know which dates were permitted and which were forbidden for weddings during the Omer (the period between the second day of Passover and the festival of Shavuoth, seven weeks later). She asked me the Sephardic and Ashkenazic customs, and showed deep concern to find a date that was appropriate according to Jewish tradition.

After we came up with a list of possible dates, I spoke with her a bit more and asked her a few questions about her forthcoming wedding. She told me that she was having the ceremony in a Catholic church, since her bridegroom was a Catholic. I asked: "If you are marrying out of the Jewish faith and are having the ceremony in a church, why did you ask me so many questions about Jewish law and tradition relating to wedding dates?" She answered: "I don't want to get married on a day that is bad luck, I want to be faithful to the Jewish tradition."

Here was a Jewish woman who had consented to marry a non-Jewish man in a church, and yet she claimed to be worried about Jewish tradition! But what was her worry? It had nothing to do with Judaism as a religious way of life: rather, it related to her superstitions about good and bad luck.

This is surely an extreme case; yet the woman's attitude is not altogether uncommon. For many, religion is viewed more as a superstition than as a way of coming closer to God. They follow certain rules and patterns not from belief or understanding or spiritual longing, but from a superstitious sense. Somehow these practices are good luck; if I do them, I will be rewarded in this world or in the next world. If I break them, I will be punished.

Carrying this idea further, people who observe the commandments of Judaism mechanically or nostalgically—but without seeking the inner spiritual meaning—are essentially operating in the realm of superstition rather than true religion. They do not see their observances as basic components in a quest for God, but as quaint folkways.

Over the years, I have met individuals who think that the mezuzah on their doorpost is a good luck charm. Indeed, some highly traditional Jews promote the idea of checking the texts in their mezuzot to see whether any letters have been erased; they think that a faulty mezuzah may lead to tragedy. I have also met individuals who, when confronted with illness, wanted amulets from holy men. Others have sought blessings from holy men, in the thought that these sages have magical qualities. Many people, who are otherwise not too fussy in their religious commitments, will become meticulous in following customs connected with mourning or the observance of death anniversaries. The tendency to superstition is strong. It is easier to engage unthinkingly in certain ritual patterns than to confront God directly.

A story is told of a barren woman who went to a Hasidic rebbe to receive a blessing from him so that she would be able to have a baby. The rebbe told her: "Pray for yourself! I will pray for you, as I pray for all who need God's help; but my prayers are no better than yours. I am not a magician." The rebbe was trying to teach genuine religion. Religion demands that individuals assume personal responsibility.

The highest of the ten sefirot of Kabbalah is Keter (crown). It suggests the loftiest possible spiritual relationship with God. It envisions each individual soul entering the throne room of the Almighty, standing alone in His presence. In this context, there are no rabbis or holy people to provide encouragement, no amulets or magical incantations, no superstitious behaviors or beliefs. This is the ultimate confrontation of a human being with God. All, as individuals, stand on their own. Alone.

The Torah states that human beings were created in the image of God. Different interpretations have been given to this phrase; for example, that human beings are rational, creative, have free will. The explanation I prefer is that humans were created with a religious instinct. The image of God within us is a spiritual drive, a longing to enter a close relationship with God. We spend our lives responding to this divine impulse. Some are successful in reaching a high spiritual level. Others get bogged down with superstitions. Still others block their spiritual drive, living their lives as though there were no God. But the image of God within each person cannot be ignored. How we respond to it largely determines who we are. If we are true to the image of God within us, we strive for the realm of Keter, the highest spiritual rung.

In giving the Torah to the people of Israel, God provided us with a path that leads to His throne. Other peoples have their own ways to follow; they, too, were created in God's image. The Jewish religious worldview neither expects nor insists that non-Jews convert to Judaism in order to achieve religious fulfillment. The Jewish hope is that all humans will recognize the One God and will live moral lives; but only Jews are bound to observe all the commandments of the Torah.

The Torah way of life is demanding. It involves prayer, study, charity, observance of a wide range of mitzvot, purity of heart and mind. In our quest for Keter, there are no shortcuts.

Rabbis, as religious leaders, are resources for those seeking to deepen their Jewish religiosity. Over the years, I have worked with many such individuals. Some had been born Jewish but were not steeped deeply enough in Torah knowledge. At some stage in their lives, they had asked themselves: What is the meaning of life? Why am I here? What is the Jewish approach to spirituality?

Sometimes, these individuals were seeking quick fixes. They wanted to study Kabbalah even though they did not even know how to read Hebrew. They asked about Jewish meditation even when they did not know the rudiments of Jewish prayer. While different people will find different starting points in their yearning for Jewish spirituality, all must ultimately come to recognize that Judaism is a way of life that demands regular study, prayer, fulfillment of mitzvot. Its highest levels can be reached only by patient, steady, devoted commitment to studying and observing the laws of Torah. It is a method of genuine spiritual growth, eschewing pseudo-spirituality, grandstanding, and superstition.

Over the years, I have spent time with earnest and sincere people who wanted to deepen their level of religious experience, who were willing to invest serious time and effort in their spiritual development. They somehow felt that their lives were not on the proper course; they longed to find their way to the path of Torah. They increased their study of Torah and their fulfillment of mitzvot. Some achieved higher religious levels, some achieved lower levels; but all were striving—knowingly or not—for the realm of Keter.

Among these individuals were some who were not halakhically Jewish, but had Jewish ancestry. They felt the call to Judaism from deep within themselves; some of them said to me, "The blood calls." I have been involved in the halakhic conversion of several people who believed themselves to be of Sephardic origin. Their ancestors were converted to Catholicism in medieval Spain and Portugal, during a period of duress for the Jews of the Iberian Peninsula. Now, these modern-day descendants wanted to return to their ancestral faith. To me, these individuals already seemed to be part of the Jewish people. Their families had been ripped away from the trunk of Jewish life, but now they were being reconnected with the Jewish tree of life. The Jewish roots had miraculously survived the generations. The conversion process was a way of officially returning them to the Jewish fold.

In May 1995, I traveled to New Mexico and Colorado to meet with individuals who believed themselves to be descendants of Spanish Jews. I spent time with groups of them, as well as in private meetings with those who so requested. Some were truly interested in coming back to their Jewish spiritual roots; others seemed more drawn by ethnicity issues; yet others were unsure of how to respond to having discovered their Jewish antecedents.

While I was in Santa Fe, we prayed in an Orthodox synagogue. Attending the morning services were Sephardic and Ashkenazic Jews, Orthodox and non-Orthodox Jews, men and women, several representatives of Lubavitch Hasidism, and some descendants of crypto-Jews who were now openly reclaiming their Jewishness. Each person in the room was the culmination of a unique historical process; that such a diverse group should pray together was a wondrous phenomenon, and all of us felt the hand of history on our shoulders. More than that, we felt the presence of God. All of us were like children who had each found our own way to the home of our Father.

People who reclaim their Jewishness travel a long journey. In the process, such individuals not only learn much for themselves, but also serve as exemplars for others. I have learned much from those of Jewish ancestry who have come to me to help them rejoin the Jewish people. Aside from those of crypto-Jewish background, I have also worked with several individuals of Donme background. Their ancestors in the seventeenth century had been followers of the pseudo-Messiah Sabbatai Zevi; when Sabbatai Zevi converted to Islam rather than face death at the order of the Turkish sultan, some of his Jewish followers also became Muslims. They came to be known as Donme (Turkish for "converts" or "apostates"), and believed that Sabbatai Zevi would ultimately return from the dead to serve as the Messiah. Although the Donme lived outwardly as Muslims, they maintained Jewish symbols and beliefs in secret. Now, a number of Donme have been seeking to return openly to the faith of their Jewish ancestors.

Many non-Jews, who lack any Jewish ancestry, have called me to discuss their desire to convert to Judaism. Some were motivated by the fact that they were interested in marrying a Jewish partner. Others had become disillusioned with the religion of their upbringing and thought they could find ultimate truth in the Torah way of life. A number of those who began the conversion process became righteous proselytes, living according to the teachings of Torah. Some went through the conversion but gradually slipped away from a life of religious commitment. Yet others never finished the conversion process. They are perpetual seekers, unable or unwilling to make a lasting commitment to one religious tradition.

Most human beings feel the need to be at home spiritually. They seek truth; they yearn for meaning; they sometimes feel lost in the cosmos. Our lives are so short in the span of eternity; the space we occupy is so infinitesimal. Life is so full of struggle and pain and betrayal. The hidden image of God within us drives us to want to be found by the Almighty, to find peace in our relationship with Him, to understand—at least on some serious level—the meaning of life.

In this quest to find and be found, prayer plays a vital role. Everyone knows instinctively how to pray, how to maintain a dialogue with God. But the ability to pray is dulled or obliterated if one does not engage in serious prayer. Prayer is an ongoing discussion with God (at least our side of the conversation); but if we stop taking part in this process, the sense of intimacy with God is lost. Synagogue ritual is a structured format that provides an ongoing framework for dialogue with God. The rabbi, as a religious teacher, not only needs to know how to pray; he also needs to know how to inspire others to open themselves to prayer. A synagogue must serve as a sanctuary, a sacred realm where people may come to think quietly, to recharge their spiritual batteries, to work on their conversation with the Almighty. It is a place where we come to find and to be found. A rabbi helps set the spiritual tone of the synagogue service. One of the best-known rabbis in Israel in recent years was known popularly as Baba Sali. The term means "our father who prays." People were drawn to him because of his genius in prayer. He conveyed a feeling of reaching toward the realm of Keter. People were better able to pray for themselves because of the inspiration they received from him.

Rabbi Joseph Soloveitchik pointed out that authentic religious expression entails a feeling of surrender to God. We pour out our souls, recognizing our smallness in the face of God's eternity and infinity. We do not come to bargain with Him or to flatter Him or to have Him do our bidding: we come as humble supplicants reminding ourselves how totally dependent we are on Him.

Some people are so spiritually sensitive that they always feel they are on the path to Keter. Others are so spiritually insensitive as not even to realize there is such a path. Yet others live their everyday lives as though there were no Keter; but from time to time they are struck by a flash of spiritual intuition. Perhaps they face a moment of truth at a time of crisis, great stress, illness, the death of a loved one. Sometimes they do not face up to Keter until they sense their own imminent demise.

The synagogue is a magnet for spiritually refined individuals who seek to enhance their religiosity. The rabbi should be a vital resource for them. But the synagogue also may attract spiritually and psychologically troubled people who view religion as a safe haven, a place to hide from personal responsibility. Or people who see religious life as a means of gaining social status. By appearing to be religious, they internalize feelings of superiority over those who are not religious. Not all the "seekers" who enter the synagogue or the rabbi's office are seeking Keter; some are really seeking ego gratification. Some people with very bad personality characteristics hide beneath the cloak of religion. The rabbi has to help these people to understand themselves so that they can reorient their thinking and behavior patterns. Many hours are spent with such individuals, but genuine progress is difficult to achieve. Their issues are not primarily religious, but psychological. They need psychiatric care more than rabbinic pastoral counseling.

The path to Keter demands a rigorous commitment to honesty with oneself. Who are we when we are alone with God? Who are we when we no longer focus on our status in society, but on our status in the throne room of the Almighty. A talmudic sage once stated: "I would rather be deemed a fool by human beings throughout my life than be deemed a fool by God if only for an instant."

While some highly spiritual individuals are able to maintain this level of insight during the course of their lifetimes, many do not achieve it except in crisis, usually when contemplating their own imminent deaths. A person who realizes that death is near has no more need for illusions and rationalizations. The moment of truth is at hand.

Dying people, once they genuinely confront the fact of their own impending death, may reach a moment of great clarity in their lives. They suddenly may seem radiant with love and wisdom, as though a tremendous burden had been lifted from their shoulders. They have reviewed their lives and have accepted the arrival of death. Over the years, I have spent time with a number of such individuals and have been profoundly moved by the experience.

Early in my rabbinic career, an elderly member of our congregation took ill and soon realized that his condition was serious. He was a pious, gentle person; he did not show fear in contemplating his impending death. Indeed, during the weeks before he died, he wrote the following lines: "I thank the Almighty for His guidance, sustenance and for the many miracles performed for me. I sincerely ask forgiveness of all my trespasses and sins. Whether conscious or not, whenever death occurs, the Shema and Hu Elohim are my last thoughts." The Shema is the classic Jewish statement proclaiming the unity of God. The Hu Elohim, which is incorporated in the liturgy of the Ten Days of Repentance between Rosh Hashanah and Yom Kippur, is a solemn declaration that the Lord is God; we believe in no false gods but only in the One God, Master of the Universe.

This gentleman was able to achieve deep inner peace and spiritual growth as he approached his death. For him, and others like him, death is part of the drive toward God. It is not a defeat, but a victory. But not everyone experiences illness and death as a step toward Keter.

Several years ago, I was called upon to minister to two individuals who were dying and knew they had little chance of surviving their illnesses. One was a religious woman in her forties, the wife of a rabbi and the mother of three children. She had fought the ravages of cancer for several years, and it had now become clear that she would not live too much longer. She was hospitalized and could no longer walk on her own. Her physical and emotional suffering were intense.

Yet, when I visited her I felt uplifted. Not only did she avoid complaining about her condition, she praised God for all the good He had bestowed upon her. She prayed that He would comfort and guide her husband and children. Her face radiated calm peacefulness. She was, of course, distressed by the prospect of her premature death, and having to be separated from her beloved family. But she drew from the wellsprings of her spiritual power, and was a source of inspiration and consolation to those who were part of her life.

The other was a man in his early seventies who had been struck by an illness that confined him to a hospital bed, with tubes in his arm and nose. This individual had led a life of prosperity and material success. His wife and children were heartbroken to see him reduced to helplessness; he had been a forceful, active, energetic man throughout his lifetime. He repeatedly told me: "I want to die with dignity." He was pained, even ashamed, of his state of helplessness. Not a particularly religious man, he found no solace in prayer or dialogue with God. He simply wanted to die as quickly as possible so as to be free of his misery.

Both suffered and died. The woman who had viewed her impending death with religious wisdom did, in fact, die with dignity. She left a legacy of faith and courage to her loved ones. The man whose life had been devoted to this-worldly concerns rather than spiritual fulfillment died as he had lived—concerned for his comfort and physical well-being.

Both of these people were good, upstanding individuals. But the different ways in which they faced their suffering and death reflect different philosophies of life and death.

A rabbi is called upon to visit the sick, eulogize the dead, comfort the mourners. He is in regular contact with those who are undergoing fundamental crises, who are struggling to understand the meaning of life, death, and suffering. The more sensitive he is, the more he learns; the more wisdom he gains, the better he is able to help and guide others. And, not least in importance, the more he can keep his own mind attuned to the transience of life and the eternity of God.

Epilogue

At the end of the talmudic tractate of Berakhot, Rabbi Hiyya bar Ashi quotes a statement in the name of Rav to the effect that rabbinic scholars have no rest—not in this world and not in the world to come. This might imply an unhappy, unsettled experience. But the Talmud goes on to explain that the reason for their inability to find rest is based on Psalms 84:8: "They go from strength to strength, every one of them appears before God in Zion." That is, they constantly are striving to reach higher levels of knowledge, wisdom, spiritual fulfillment. Whether in this world or the next world, they go from strength to strength, seeking to appear before God.

Such an existence implies feelings of failure and imperfection. It suggests that we always can be and should be reaching for higher levels. Even if we have attained strength, we need to go on to a yet greater strength.

Life is a spiritual ladder, beginning with the perception of God's kingship in the universe. We climb, and fall, and try again. We advance one rung, we hesitate, we regress, we advance another rung. Life is a powerful drama, never a complete success, rarely a complete failure.

A rabbinic homily has it that a human life is like a book. We each write our own story, some better, some worse.

The true worth of the book is not known until it is completed; and even then it may not be properly evaluated by human beings. But God is the True Judge.

What is a rabbi? He is a person who occupies himself with assorted tasks and responsibilities on behalf of Judaism and the Jewish people. He accomplishes various things, accumulates certain honors, fills certain functions.

Who is a rabbi? He is one who finds no rest in this world and expects to find no rest in the world to come. He is one who strives mightily—and often without success—to go from strength to strength.

Bibliography

This book is indebted to numerous authors whose works I have read over the years. The following bibliography includes items mentioned in this book, or which have had a clear and overt influence on my thinking about this book. It also includes a listing of books written and edited by me, since each of these projects has played its role in my rabbinic life.

Angel, Marc D., trans. and ed. *The Essential Pele Yoetz.* New York: Sepher Hermon Press. 1991.

———, ed. *Exploring Sephardic Customs and Traditions.* Hoboken: Ktav. 2000.

———, ed. *Exploring the Thought of Rabbi Joseph B. Soloveitchik.* Hoboken: Ktav. 1997.

———, ed. *From Strength to Strength.* New York: Sepher Hermon Press. 1998.

———, ed. *Haham Gaon Memorial Volume.* New York: Sepher Hermon Press and Sephardic House. 1997.

———. *The Jews of Rhodes.* New York: Sepher Hermon Press and Union of Sephardic Congregations. 1978. (Reprinted 1980; 1998).

———. *La America: The Sephardic Experience in the United States.* Philadelphia: Jewish Publication Society. 1982.

———. *Loving Truth and Peace: The Grand Religious Worldview of Rabbi Benzion Uziel.* Northvale: Jason Aronson. 1999.

———. *The Orphaned Adult: Confronting the Death of a Parent.* New York: Human Sciences Press. 1987. (Reprinted by Jason Aronson, 1997).

———, ed. *Rabbi David de Sola Pool: Selections from Six Decades of Sermons, Addresses and Writings.* New York: Union of Sephardic Congregations. 1980.

———. *The Rhythms of Jewish Living.* New York: Sepher Hermon Press and Sephardic House. 1986. (Reprinted by Jason Aronson, 1997).

———. *Seeking Good, Speaking Peace: Collected Essays of Rabbi Marc D. Angel* (edited by Rabbi Hayyim Angel). Hoboken: Ktav. 1994.

———, trans. and ed. *A Sephardic Passover Haggadah.* Hoboken: Ktav. 1988.

———. *Sephardi Voices 1492-1992: A Study Guide.* New York: Hadassah. 1991.

———, ed. *Studies in Sephardic Culture.* New York: Sepher Hermon Press and Sephardic House. 1980.

———. *Voices in Exile: A Study in Sephardic Intellectual History.* Hoboken: Ktav. 1991.

Arieti, Silvano. *The Will to Be Human.* New York: Quadrangle Books. 1972.

Berlin, Isaiah. "The Pursuit of the Ideal," in *The Proper Study of Mankind.* New York: Farrar, Straus and Giroux. 1997. Pages 1-16.

Buber, Martin. *I and Thou.* New York: Charles Scribner's Sons. 1970.

Frankl, Viktor. *Man's Search for Meaning*. New York: Washington Square Press. 1985.

Halevy, Haim David. *Asei Lekha Rav*. 9 vols. Tel Aviv. 5736-5749.

———. *Mayyim Hayyim*. 3 vols. Tel Aviv. 5751-5758.

Kaplan, Aryeh. *Jewish Meditation*. New York: Schocken Books. 1985.

Lamm, Norman. "Tzeniut: A Universal Concept," in *Haham Gaon Memorial Volume*. New York: Sepher Hermon Press and Sephardic House. 1997. pages 151-162.

Neihardt, John. *Black Elk Speaks*. New York: Pocket Books. 1972.

Rakeffet-Rothkoff, Aaron. *The World of Rabbi Joseph B. Soloveitchik*. 2 vols. Hoboken: Ktav. 1999.

Soloveichik, Joseph B. *Besod ha-Yahid ve-ha-Yahad*. ed. Pinchas Peli. Jerusalem. 5736.

———. "The Community", in *Tradition,* 17:2, 1978. (Also in this issue, "Majesty and Humility"; "Redemption, Prayer and Talmud Torah"; "A Tribute to the Rebbitzen of Talne.")

———. *Halakhic Man* (translated by Lawrence Kaplan). Philadelphia: Jewish Publication Society. 1983.

———. "The Lonely Man of Faith," in *Tradition,* 7:2, 1965.

Steinsaltz, Adin. The Thirteen Petalled Rose. New York: Basic Books. 1980.

Uziel, Benzion. *Mishpetei Uziel*. 7 vols. Tel Aviv and Jerusalem, 5695-5724.

———. *Mikhmanei Uziel*. Tel Aviv. 5699.

———. *Hegyonei Uziel*. 2 vols. Jerusalem. 5713-5714.

Watts, Alan. *The Supreme Identity*. New York. 1972.